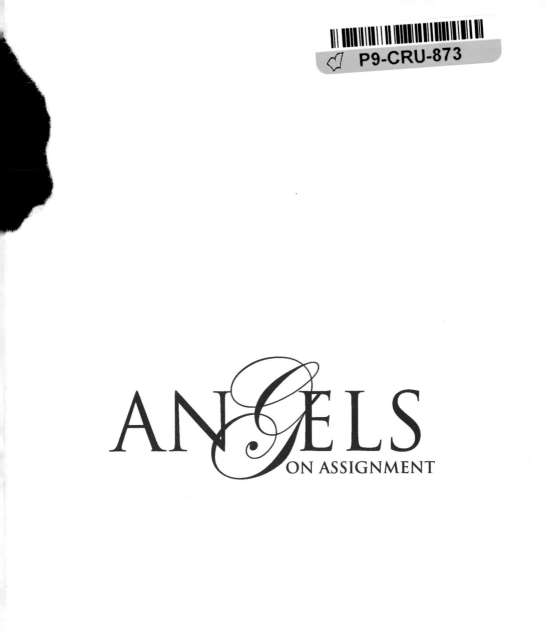

ANGELS
ON ASSIGNMENT

ANGELS
ON ASSIGNMENT

ROLAND BUCK

W

WHITAKER
HOUSE

ANGELS ON ASSIGNMENT
Second Edition

Cassette tapes by Roland Buck are available from:
Buck Ministries Tape Dept.
12000 Fairview Ave.
Boise, ID 83713

ISBN-13: 978-0-88368-697-3
ISBN-10: 0-88368-697-X
Printed in the United States of America
© 1979 by Roland H. Buck

1030 Hunt Valley Circle
New Kensington, PA 15068
www.whitakerhouse.com

Library of Congress Cataloging-in-Publication Data

Buck, Roland.
Angels on assignment / Roland Buck.—2nd ed.
p.   cm.
ISBN-10: 0-88368-697-X (trade pbk. : alk. paper)
ISBN-13: 978-0-88368-697-3 (trade pbk. : alk. paper)
1. Angels. 2. Buck, Roland. 3. Gabriel (Archangel) 4. Private revelations. I. Title.
BT966.3.B83 2004
235'.3—dc22
2004027070

3 4 5 6 7 8 9 10 11 12 **W** 15 14 13 12 11 10 09 08

Contents

A WORD FROM THE WIFE
OF
ROLAND BUCK

What an exciting day to be alive! Although we have the darkness of wickedness on every hand, we have the assurance of God caring through a great supernatural renewal in our day.

A spiritual awakening is always characterized by miracles of healing, many conversions and a new touch in lives.

Part of the special work God is doing is a broader revelation of himself through the messages brought by angelic visitation.

To think that our family and church could be a part of this expression of his love is more than I can comprehend.

Two questions people ask me when they know that my precious husband has had many angelic enounters are: "Have you seen an angel," and "Why did God choose your husband?"

I have not yet had an angelic encounter, but at times when I have gone to bed at night I have experienced such an overwhelming inflow of God's presence that I have had to go downstairs to praise and worship him. I am very much at peace because I know God does everything right. My husband is the leader and the one who is ministering to the people, so God has laid his hand especially on him. Who am I to question God? Our love is so close and we share the ministry so much together that although I have not seen an angel, I have been abundantly blessed as my husband pours out to me the truths that God has shown to him.

In answer to the second question, "Why did God choose him?" you must understand my evaluations are purely human because we cannot limit God.

In the first place, my husband is not easily swayed. We have pastored in Boise, Idaho, for 29 years. Through the years I have seen such a confidence and trust in God that he has been like a rock of Gibraltar.

He has maintained a steady, even ministry in spite of so-called "fads" in religious circles — not "swayed with every wind of doctrine," but weighing carefully those things which could be of a questionable nature.

He has always been a great student of the Word and in his ministry has built a bridge for the unbeliever instead of a barrier to the kingdom of God.

The angelic encounters have not been his first knowledge of God dealing with him in a special way. Many times he has come to bed in the morning after God has spoken to him through the night hours regarding truths in the Word, giving him many scriptures to bear out the particular message he wanted to give him.

His consistency and stability have created within me and our four children a trust in God that is unwavering. He has suffered three heart attacks and one heart arrest, but through it all the peace of God was felt within our whole family. God has given us a wonderful heritage.

Although my husband has meditated a great deal on the Word, he is not a mystic, but very human and a person I have grown to love and trust.

God can do as he pleases. Didn't he visit many people in the Old and New Testaments? He is still able to do the same in these days — God is the God of the supernatural — who can deny it?

Charmian Buck

ENCOUNTER

Possibly the questions most often asked are . . .

"How did it happen that God chose you?"

"Was it through deep hunger on your part?"

"Was it through prayer and fasting?"

I would honestly have to say . . . "I don't know! I fall short in all of these areas!"

CHAPTER I

ENCOUNTER

The most outstanding and thrilling thing that has ever taken place in my life has been the angelic visitations which have occurred during the last two years.

God made it very clear to me that I am to share what happened in my life, so I am passing on descriptions of what I have seen, experiences I have had, and messages I have been given.

God is illuminating truths of the Bible in unprecedented ways prior to the return of Jesus. Revelations are being brought forth in all ministries flowing in the Spirit. In this relation, God quickened my spirit to John 16:12-15: "Oh, there is so much more I want to tell you, but you can't understand it now. When the Holy Spirit, who is truth, comes, he shall guide you into all truth, for he will not be presenting his own ideas, but will be passing on to you what he has heard. He will tell you about the future" (TLB). These words were spoken by Jesus.

I have written these encounters and messages with the limitation of my own human understanding. In doing this, I have made references to what the angels have said, but not with the thought of quoting them verbatim, except where I have so stated. When you consider that there have been some fifty hours of angelic conversation which I have condensed with my own words and understanding into this single volume, you can perhaps realize that I have relied on my human ability to express these truths as I have comprehended them. I have not added to, or taken away from the Word of God, but the Spirit has opened my eyes to things I had not previously seen, just as he reveals truths to any believer who searches the Word.

Among the many agencies the Spirit uses to minister to us are the Bible, circumstances, other believers and angels. He speaks directly to us in many ways — through dreams, visions, and gifts of the Spirit, but always, it is the same Holy Spirit who speaks to us. "Our words are wise because they are from God . . . But we know about these things because God has sent his Spirit to tell us, and his Spirit searches out and shows us all of God's deepest secrets" (I Cor. 2:7, 10 TLB).

Paul also referred to receiving messages from God when he said, "Yet when I am among mature Christians I do speak with words of great wisdom, but not the kind that comes from here on earth, and not the kind that appeals to the great men of this world, who are doomed to fall" (I Cor. 2:6 TLB). Praise God he is still speaking to us today!

I know there are risks involved in speaking of unusual and uncommon experiences such as these. My first reaction was to try to get out of giving the message brought to me by an angel. I valued my credibility and felt it would be shattered. You will discover in these writings that God helped me change my mind.

Some have asked what has happened as a result of these messages. Needless to say, I have no way of measuring the total impact, but evidence abounds that the Holy Spirit, true to his promise, has given wings to these messages and they have circled the globe by tape cassettes. People in all parts of the world have been liberated by these fresh truths from God's heart. Thousands have accepted Christ. Thousands of others who had given up, have been renewed. A number of pastors with whom I am personally acquainted had become discouraged and left the ministry. Today, because they have found new hope, they have returned to a place of service. As the Spirit accompanying these messages made the words they were hearing come alive, a new door of faith has opened wide to believers everywhere!

At the time of this writing, there have been sixteen separate visitations by angels. Though they come often, every two or three weeks, I have not, and cannot, become accustomed to them. There is such a holiness and such an awesomeness connected with each visit, that every time I see them, I am reminded of the eternal and unchanging God who has sent them, his closeness to us, and his intense interest and loving concern for our families.

Each time the angels have come, they have brought a message from God for the world. If I could put the substance of these messages into one simple phrase, it would have to be, "I CARE!"

As you read, I would encourage you to look beyond the encounter to the message. How very important each one must be to God for him to send them by "special" messenger. The messages included in this book have been given to my church following each one of the encounters. They are not angelic quotations as such, but a sharing of truths made real.

It might be of interest to you to know that during the two to four hours they have stayed each time they have come, there has not been one verse of Scripture quoted. Instead, a living panorama causes truth to literally come alive as it passes before me. At times I have found myself living what I was seeing. Not once did they leave without giving me Bible references where the message could be found.

Because of the nature of this book, some may look for reasons to refuse to accept . . . instead of reasons why God has sent these messages. To others it may be in conflict with accepted beliefs. This is understandable. God merely stated how things really are, and made no effort to support any chosen position or theology, but rather to reveal his deep love for a world that had lost its way, but has been found as a result of the sacrifice of Jesus.

Possibly the questions asked most often are, "How did it happen that God chose you?" "Was it through deep hunger on your part?" "Was it through prayer and fasting?" I would honestly have to say, "I don't know!" I fall short in all of these areas.

The activity of angels will intrigue you, but a word of caution was brought from God by Gabriel: "Do not seek angels. Seek Jesus! He is far greater than any angel!"

GOOD NEWS FOR YOU AND YOUR FAMILY

Do you know . . .

That if even one member of your family is living for God, each individual member is highly favored?

That a great host of angels has been assigned to bring these highly favored people to God?

That they have orders to listen to no objections, but to hasten individuals to a point of choice?

That if a person chooses the wrong way, the angels will begin the cycle all over again?

CHAPTER 2

GOOD NEWS FOR YOU AND YOUR FAMILY

On the night of June 18, 1978, I went to bed at my usual time with no advance notice that something was about to happen which would change my entire life!

About three o'clock in the morning, I was abruptly awakened when someone grasped my arms and sat me right up in bed! The room was dark because the shades were pulled, but there was just enough light from outside so I could detect the outline of a huge being.

To say the least, I was frightened because he was so strong I couldn't free myself from his grip. My fear didn't last, however, because I quickly became aware of a supernatural presence, and it didn't take me long to realize that this heavenly being was an angel from God. He confirmed this, turned loose of my shoulders, and told me not to be afraid! Then he told me that God had sent him because the prayers of God's people had been heard, and he was to deliver the message that their prayers had not only been heard, but had been answered! Hallelujah! I wasn't dreaming, it wasn't a vision, it was something very, very real!

As we continued talking, he spoke so loudly I was sure he was going to wake up my wife who was asleep next to me. He didn't, but I wish he had!

My dog, Queenie, comes into our room once in awhile when she gets lonesome, and sleeps beside the bed. She was there that night and was interested in everything the angel had to say. She was right beside me and I could feel her head turning every which way against my leg as first the angel spoke and then I answered! It was an unusual visit!

It sounds strange, and I imagine some people might question my credibility. This is not important; God's message is, and he had something he wanted me to bring to the world!

This unique conversation lasted for two solid hours as the angel shared magnificent truths from the Word of God with me. He discussed the unfolding plan of God for the entire world and brought me warm feelings from God's own heart as to the concern he has for people. His love for people is so great, he is a lot more interested in them than he is in procedure! He LOVES people!

The angel gave me information which went in many, many different directions, but there was a keynote which the Lord emphasized to me that followed all the way through, and at first I wasn't certain how to relate this message until one night three weeks later, he returned, bringing more beautiful truths from God on the same subjects. I wanted to see what he looked like, but again I could only see the outline of this heavenly being in the darkness of our bedroom.

The morning following the second visit, my wife asked me if we had had another visitor during the night, because she said while she did not hear anything, she was aware of the real warmth of God's presence filling the room.

There is something so awesome about God sending these special messengers with words from heaven that I feel a tremendous responsibility in sharing this. We are living in a beautiful time and a great awakening is happening throughout the world. Along with the great move of the Holy Spirit, there are also renewed attacks by the enemy against the work of God.

In an effort to get at God and to try to hurt him, satanic forces are attacking the home, which is the closest thing on earth to God's heart. Homes are hurting and many times they do not understand why. This attack is more than just an attack on the home for every time you find a new chapter about to be opened in God's great work, you will find increased satanic activity. The enemies of God are following a practice that began a long time ago.

In talking about these satanic attacks, the angel brought to my mind the ways the enemy fought in times past. When Moses was born and the plan of God began to unfold so that the children of Israel would be brought out of the land of Egypt, God prepared a small child whose mother recognized that he was very special and Satan made an effort to fight against God's plan.

Satan didn't know whom God had chosen, so he put it into the heart of the king to kill every child below a certain age so that he could get rid of the one baby who was going to have a definite part in the unfolding of God's plan.

Another time was when a decree was given in Shushan. The enemy knew that the time was almost here for the great deliverance of Israel, so he worked through the heart of a man named Haman. A decree went out that all of the Jews were to be slain. Again the enemy tried to stop God's plan, but he did not succeed.

When Jesus was born, the greatest chapter of all times began to unfold. Again the satanic forces said, "We have to stop him. He is God's own Son. We have to stop this deliverer, but we don't know where he is." They inquired, "Where is he? Where is he going to be born?"

If Satan could have read minds, all he would have had to do was to go to the shepherds or the wise men and read their minds, but they weren't telling! He discovered the general area, so that same satanic force went into operation. Once again all the babies were killed. But Jesus wasn't there!

In our day, there is a beautiful new chapter unfolding as God is bringing into focus the families of the earth. He is letting them know that his plan of salvation, a principle he put into operation years and years ago, is not just a plan for a single person. He reserves a place for the whole family, but each member must individually be born again.

I thought, "That's strange theology! That doesn't seem right." But I discovered that God himself is the one who started this! It was in his beautiful plan that he gave to Moses in the tabernacle. The angel brought to my attention the fact that God wanted the name of every head of the house and his family included in the gate of the tabernacle; the silver sockets, which held the veil of the temple, were to be made out of the shekels of their redemption. These sacrifices of half a shekel of silver were made by each man as a ransom for his soul unto the Lord. The shekels were to be melted, and the gates were to hang on the very fact that God has included ALL in his plan.

This redemption plan for the families was so important to God that he required each family to give a memorial offering of half a shekel every year so they wouldn't forget. This is discussed in Exodus 30:12-16 and 38:25-28.

Do you remember when Rahab saved the spies who went into Jericho? The spies, by inspiration of God, said, "Rahab, call your family here to this house and they will all be saved." God worked through the one person that he had contact with in that home. Rahab brought every member of her family there, and they were all saved because God cared for the entire family!

God's plan is a family plan. All of the beautiful ties of home and family are eternal, and you are going to have joy such as you have never dreamed of when you get to heaven. Gabriel spoke to me over and over again about the importance of families to God, and that we can trust him, even though we cannot comprehend how he can accomplish a family relationship in heaven. "How impossible it is for us to understand his decisions and his methods!" (Rom. 11:33 TLB).

The enemy wants to spoil God's plan by hurling heavy artillery into the homes, causing husbands to lose feelings for their wives; causing restlessness; causing things to fall apart; causing children and parents to hate each other. But God says Satan is not going to get away with it!

One of the most impressive things the angel told me was that God always has a back-up plan. God says his work will get done even if he has to call in someone else to do it — or he will do it himself!

This is beautifully described in the story of Esther, when Mordecai came to her and prophetically told her that God had put her right there at that particular time to get a job done. She could choose to do it if she wanted to, and be really blessed of God, but she could also be confident that his deliverance was not going to fail if she decided not to do it (Esther 4:14). God's plan will go through and he will raise up deliverance from another source if necessary. He will not fail!

God let me know that events which he has decreed HAVE TO HAPPEN! When he decrees it, an irreversible force is set in motion that nothing can stop. IT HAS TO HAPPEN! People he has included in his unfolding plan are not irreversibly stuck with that plan for themselves unless they want to be. God has predestined the event, but not the individuals. He said, "If you will link arms with me, there will be joy and happiness in it for you. I have FOREORDAINED you to be a partner with me in the great work that I am doing, but I will not hold you to it."

God is at work! The enemy is at work! These are the two opposing forces, but God has already decreed that he is the winner!

Many Christians have been praying for the unsaved loved ones in their families. When the angel brought me the message that their prayers had already been answered, I thought, "Does this mean they are already ALL saved?" "No, God does not mean he will violate the free right of choice he has given, but it means that he is going to do everything necessary to bring people to the point where it will be easy for them to make the choice to serve him.

I have heard it said, "It's a good thing to make it hard for people to come to God because that way they will appreciate him." That isn't God's way! He wants to make it real easy to come to him, and real hard to get away! His whole desire is for you. He loves you! He's not looking for some reason to cast you away. He is looking for every reason to hold you!

Since God has said that your prayers are already answered, those who have laid their loved ones before him in sincerity and in faith can stop praying right now! The angel said they can start praising God right now. He is on the job, and has released the forces to bring about circumstances which would make it hard for these people to resist God.

Then the angel said, "I am here right now leading a great band of angels in order to clear the way, to scatter the enemies, to move away the roadblocks, and to let people know that the heart of God is warm toward them."

He shared many beautiful truths with me, and on this particular visit as he spoke to me, I realized the angel was the same one who had appeared to Zacharias with an identical message, "Your prayers are heard!" (Luke 1:13).

This message that God brought to me through his angel was a little picture of the big heart of God and what he is doing today. The angel told me that God was interested in restoring homes into the kind of unit that would please him and that he could bless. He said his desire was to restore communication between children and their parents, and break down barriers of hatred so they could be buddies and have a wonderful family relationship.

God showed his keen interest in families by forming the home before he made the church. He wants that same wonderful unity, and that recognition of himself, which people expect to feel only in the church, to also be in the home.

He said, "I want the fathers to feel the hurts of their family. I want the children to know that when the enemy attacks, they can find a strong arm at home on which to lean. I want the mothers' hearts to be opened and filled with compassion for the kids." I was certainly aware of the fact that God was interested in families, but to have an angel tell me this made it more real!

He said that God's purpose, his desire, and one of the things that he wants to accomplish in all that he is doing, is to reach the rebellious children. He wants to turn the hearts of fathers and mothers toward their children. He said, "I want to take those rebellious children, those who are disobedient, and bring them to a point of knowing how complete my forgiveness really is. I want them to know that when they obey me, there is not one thing from the past against them on their record up in heaven. When I forgive, I not only forget the thing for which I have forgiven them, but I even forget that I forgave!

When you come to God the next time and say, "God, I hate to keep coming, because I know this is the twentieth time you have forgiven me, but will you forgive me once again?" He will look at you and say, "What are you talking about? I do not have any record of that. I do not have anything in my memory about that. As far as I'm concerned, this is the first time you have come." Did you know that this is the kind of forgiveness God has?

I have heard many messages on how beautiful it is that God justifies the godly people, and I think this is wonderful! But God goes a step further, and says, "I want you to carry the message that I am ready to justify the ungodly" (Rom. 4:5).

The word justify means "just as though it had never happened." God said, "Because of the snares and the attacks of the devil, I want my people to know how complete that justification really is! I want to go into their minds, their hearts, and into their well-being. I want them to be able to look up into my face and know that they do not have to hang their heads and be ashamed, because when I see them, I see them as first-class members of my family."

He told me that I could find a brief of this message in Luke 1:17. This was the time of another great unfolding of a chapter in his plan. I got out my Bible to read it to see if it really said it that way, and lo and behold, it says it just that way. He was speaking about John the Baptist and the anointing of the Spirit and how John was going to go out and do God's work. "He shall go before him in the spirit and power of Elias, to turn the hearts of the fathers to the children, and the disobedient (or rebellious) to the wisdom of the just; to make ready a people prepared for the Lord." He wanted to let them know experientially what justification really means. God wants you to know that he is not your enemy; he is your friend! He doesn't want to hurt you; he wants to help you!

Then he reminded me of something that happened in Acts 27:20 where Paul was shipwrecked. I really got excited when I read this! A terrible storm came up and all hope was gone. The crew gave up in despair, because they felt they would not be saved. But, in verse 22, Paul said, "I exhort you to be of good cheer: for there shall be no loss of any man's life among you, but of the ship." How did Paul know this? ". . . For there stood by me this night the angel of God, whose I am, and whom I serve, Saying, Fear not, Paul; thou must be brought before Caesar: (God's plan was unfolding, and he was not going to allow anything like a storm to stop those plans) and, lo, God hath given thee all them that sail with thee."

To you parents, God is saying the same thing, "I'm giving you all those who are sailing with you."

When he said, "Wherefore, sirs, be of good cheer: (I've got good news for you) for I believe God, that it shall be even as it was told me."

It shall be just the way the angel said it!

Paul told them to stand by, but many of the people didn't believe him. I'm sure some of them thought, "Man, this guy's had hallucinations. We have been in the storm area for too many days." They had seen men lose their minds before, because of the storms. They said, "We can hear the ground under the ship; we have sounded down."

So with the guise of throwing some anchors over, they threw a boat over, and were going to get into it, but Paul said, "You had better obey. God has plans to save you, but you have to make the choice yourself." The soldiers cut the rope and the boat fell into the water.

God still had a plan, and he sent a host of angels and they took the back end of the ship, twisted it off, and broke it up into little pieces so everyone would have something to hang onto. The angel visitor said that he had led a host of angels in at that time to make sure each person got to shore. Each one of the 276 who were saved had a big angel watching over them!

I asked the angel, "Wouldn't it have been better if they had drowned, since they were a pretty rough bunch of characters? They were prisoners, many of them murderers, and humans of the lowest kind." No, the great miracle happened because God wants to save! Jesus didn't come to condemn the world, but that the world through him might have life!

I think of the reluctance I had in delivering the first message that was brought to me. I didn't know where it was going to go! I didn't know what it was going to do! I have spent twenty-nine years in my community endeavoring to share Christ with the people; the community recognizes my ministry; it is accepted, and I didn't want to destroy the work of a lifetime in one evening by telling an experience that would cause defenses to rise, and turn people away.

The angel told me to give the message, but I could not. I waited three weeks, and in the middle of the night, those same strong hands that had grasped my arms before, raised me up in bed and said, "You haven't given that message." I knew I was in trouble! I was still reluctant, so I asked the angel, "Since you are here, why don't I introduce you to the people and let you give the message to them?" He replied that God would not permit him to, so I had to give it myself.

I was especially cautious when I gave this message in church because the angel was there, making sure I gave the entire message. He said, "Even though I will not give the message to the congregation, I want you to know that I am here, and I have a whole army of angels with me right now." It really excited me to know that angels were in the service! Then he said there were more angels there that night than people! How I wish we could have crystallized them to make them visible.

Because God is rapidly moving forward to accomplish his plan on schedule, Satan is also working hard. He wants to spoil what God is doing, but God said he is not going to succeed.

In Numbers 10:35 we read that when the cloud moved, and the ark and the people were ready to move ahead, Moses said, "Rise up, Lord, and let thine enemies be scattered." God showed him when to say it. There were a lot of enemies lurking along the way, and when Moses gave the signal, the angelic hosts of heaven swung into action and swooped out across the area where Moses and the Israelites would be traveling, clearing the way of all enemies, whether spiritual or physical.

Did you know that you are on God's special list because somebody in your family loves Jesus and they are asking God to save you? Even if you have not yet given him your life, a host of angels has already come! He has already given the cry, "Enemies be scattered!" There are angels working to bring you out of the enemy camp into God's safety. They are pushing things out of the way because God said that you are highly favored.

If you have been praying for a family member who does not know the Lord, and have sincerely laid them on the altar, stop pestering them! Quit preaching at them! They're getting enough pushing and pulling right now from the angels, and the Holy Spirit is doing a thorough job of preaching to them.

One of the big angels who later talked to me said he was the same one who was standing beside Joshua when Joshua said, "Are you on our side, or the enemies' side?" The angel replied, "You are wrong on both counts, but I have come as the leader of another army and we are taking our orders from heaven. Your God, who is giving those orders, knows what the needs are."

There's an army at work right now. Wherever men and women honestly lay their loved ones out before God, those names are written on a very special list. This does not mean that God is going to stop only with those families, God is reaching people and drawing them in from all walks of life.

In Psalm 89:33-37 we read about that very special list where God said he would make an everlasting covenant with us, even the sure mercies of David. Then he tells us what the sure mercies of David are, that if your children drift away from God, they are going to get into trouble. "Then will I visit their transgression with the rod, and their iniquity with stripes" (Ps. 89:32).

They are going to have a rough time, but nevertheless, because I made a promise to you, "my lovingkindness will I not utterly take from him, nor suffer my faithfulness to fail" (Ps. 89:33). He is going to stay right on them, encouraging them to come back to his family.

I didn't ask this angel to identify himself, or to give any credentials. But, he said, "To set your mind at ease as to the authenticity of this visit, to erase any doubts from your mind, I want to give you some scripture references where I am referred to in God's Word, and it's settled there!" and that is what he did! He was the angel who was with Zacharias, with Paul at the shipwreck, with Moses to scatter the enemies, and with Joshua.

Again today I can hear the battle cry, "Rise up, Lord. Let your enemies be scattered," and already the angels have moved out for action!

When I gave this first message to my church, God gave me a confirmation that it was from him! Someone took the tape of GOOD NEWS and gave it to a friend who was visiting here from Canada. About two o'clock one Saturday morning, my wife answered the phone and as she handed it to me said, "Someone is really crying and I can't make sense out of him." I told the man on the other end of the line to take it easy so I could understand him. He said, "I'm up here in Canada, and somebody brought me a tape of yours. A bunch of us decided we would have a big party tonight, and have a lot of fun laughing at someone who was talking about angels.

"We thought this would be the funniest thing ever, so we all got together and went to the saloon. We got our jugs of beer and sat around the table. We were going to play the tape over and over and just have a big time laughing! We thought it would be a real blast! We turned the tape recorder on, but none of us touched our beer! In about five minutes, a few of us started crying, and then others started crying. There were seventeen of us together in the saloon.

"We played it over three times and someone said, 'What are we going to do, we've got to do something!' " They couldn't figure out what to do. It was like they were in a daze. Finally one of them said, "Why don't we call him — that pastor." So they called the operator and got my number. When he related the story about listening to the tape, he pleadingly asked me, "What are we going to do?"

I said, "God has followed that tape to Canada with his angels, and he wants you to turn your life over to him. Just slip your hand into his right now."

After the man prayed with me over the telephone, he said, "My life is beginning right today. I'm going back and tell those other sixteen what to do and get them all to turn their lives over to God!" Hallelujah!

I had six calls the first week which confirmed to me that this message was from God and that I was to share it with the world. Not one of the individuals who called me knew who I was, and none of them had heard the tape except the man from Canada.

Another time the phone rang early one morning, and it was a man calling from Wyoming. He said, "I feel like an idiot. I don't know what I'm calling you for."

"Well, what are you calling me for, waking me up in the middle of the night like this?"

"You may not believe this, but tonight I heard a loud voice say, 'Call Pastor Buck in Boise, Idaho.'" He said he thought he was losing his mind so he ignored the order and in a few minutes he heard that same voice again say with great authority, "I want you to call Pastor Buck in Boise, Idaho!"

There was so much pressure on him, he finally called the operator to see if there was a Pastor Buck in Boise, Idaho. He said, "They gave me your number, so here I am. I don't know what I called you for, but I was told to call you, so here I am."

I KNEW THE ANGELS HAD BEEN BUSY!

"I know why you called," I said, and led him to the Lord. Then I asked him, "Is there someone in your family, a relative perhaps, who knows God?"

"I have a "nutty" sister who knows God, or says she knows him. I've been listening to her, but I didn't believe her!"

"Because of this nutty sister, you are highly favored of God. God made a promise that he was going to stay right on you and he didn't let up until you were saved!"

It was a real joy when another man stopped by who had been troubled about his sister who didn't know the Lord. When he heard about angels going out to bring people to the ones who would minister salvation to them, he got down on his knees and said, "Lord, I'm going to lay my sister and my family out before you, and I'm going to praise you for what you are going to do." That very week his sister found Jesus as her Savior and Lord, and now God is working on the rest of the members of the family.

Reports are coming in from all over that these angels are bringing people to the place where they can make a decision for Christ. God's messages and his salvation are snowballing around the world.

The angel re-emphasized the fact to me that these ministering angels were out working and bringing people to those who would minister salvation to them. Again he emphasized the fact that we must prepare ourselves and be alert to help those who will come to us. Then he said, "You have accepted the teaching that Jesus is the door and the way. You are bringing people to the door," he said, "but God wants you to know that you are also a door." When Jesus said, "As my Father sent me, so send I you," he dispatched us exactly as he is. We are a door to Christ, and he is the door to God.

Jesus said, "Verily, verily, I say unto you, He that believeth on me, the works that I do shall he do also; and greater works than these shall he do; because I go unto my Father" (John 14:12). He has not only given us the Holy Spirit, but he gave us his job to do!

Jesus, as a human channel of God, was the door through which people found God. "And Christ became a human being and lived here on earth among us ..." (John 1:14 TLB). People who can't find Jesus in this world can find us! Today many people are going out and becoming a door, or a channel, through which others are finding Christ as their Savior.

Jesus said, "I am the light of the world," in John 8:12, and in Matt. 5:14 he said, "Ye are the light of the world." This does not give deity to man, because we are not Jesus, but we are the human doors and "the light of the world" which he uses on this earth! He wants us to take this same kind of authority that these angels are taking and not listen to anyone's objections when they come to us.

As the Spirit draws and calls people, they often refuse to listen, and strenuously object, but the angels don't listen.

They have orders to bring people to a point of either accepting or rejecting Jesus. If they refuse, the angels start the cycle over again, and again, and again as directed by the Spirit.

Not everyone who comes your way will be brought by the Spirit, but God wants you to be sensitive enough to hear the words they are saying, or sense their discouragement. We are to let them know the angels are at work and they cannot dispose of them just by turning away and refusing to listen. If they do, the angels will start the cycle right over again! And if they refuse again, the angels will start once more. Angels do not get discouraged. They are taking all their orders from heaven. Praise God!

We can speak in Jesus' name because we have his authority. When someone sincerely says, "Jesus, I accept you," it is our responsibility to let them know that God has accepted them. God has given us this authority through Jesus. We are his representatives! We can say this, because God will back us up in everything we do that is according to his Word. "Whosoever you free," he said, "I am going to free."

God's Good News for you today is that God is vitally interested in each person and in families, and that he is even sending angelic messengers to bring those who are away from him into his own family. He really loves people!

MINISTRY OF ANGELS

The light flipped on and I saw what appeared to be two of the largest men I had ever seen!

Strong currents of radiation pulsated from them. I started to fall, but was steadied by the strong hand of these seven-foot-plus beings. IT SOUNDED LIKE HE SAID, "I AM GABRIEL," but it couldn't be . . . he has not been seen for centuries.

Am I really seeing things or IS HE REALLY HERE . . . IN MY HOME?

CHAPTER 3

MINISTRY OF ANGELS

Through the inspiring messages brought by angels, the Lord has given me some beautiful insights that I could never have learned by intensive study. When God brought these exciting truths to me, he did not say, "See if you can tailor these to fit into your doctrinal concepts. See if you can fit them into the position you have chosen." He doesn't even act like he knows of any positions! He just said, "This is what is going to happen!"

In the awesomeness of the presence of God's angels, I have often felt like Mary, who said, "May everything you said come true" (Lk. 1:38 TLB). When Paul said, ". . . There stood by me this night the angel of God, whose I am, and whom I serve" (Acts 27:23), he knew it would come to pass! In the same way, I KNOW that these messages which have come from God's heart are continually robbing hell of its future inhabitants.

These truths are vital and real! The mere presence of these magnificent angelic beings, who come right from the throne of God, is so awesome I could never criticize any person for falling flat on his face before one! I would not even criticize those few people in the Bible who had a desire to worship them, even though they did not!

These angels have made simple, basic truths become alive and real to me! They have highlighted, and brought into focus, certain scriptures which could never have been opened to me any other way. These are simple Bible principles which God has allowed me to view through his

eyes, but I certainly did not bypass the Bible in order to
see them. God put them there a long time ago, but scales
on our spiritual eyes have prevented us from seeing them.

Every truth these angelic beings have made real to me,
has been supported by the Word of God. After these
glorious revelations, difficult truths become simple! How
could I have missed them all this time? They are so plain
and so beautiful, and every one of these messages highlights
the sacrifice of Jesus, for the angels never speak of God's
eternal plan without mentioning his death. It's always in
the message, somewhere, that beautiful, complete sacrifice
of Jesus!

I spent some time musing about these things. You can
well understand that you cannot close the door to an
overwhelming experience like this, take it out of your mind
and say, "Well, now, that's that! I got the message! I've
had this experience, and now we will move on to the next
phase!"

It is totally impossible! The awesomeness of the experience, and the overwhelming presence of God, are things I
cannot put out of my mind even when I close my eyes at
night. Because of these angelic visits, there is a sub-
conscious awareness of God, his presence, and his reality at
all times. One of the greatest things to me about these
visitations has been the fact that they have let people know
that God lives, and he hasn't forgotten them.

I do not know if I will ever have another angelic visit.
However, these visits have had enough impact on my life
that nothing on this earth, or even in heaven, could take
what this has done from my heart and my mind! God is
preparing people, and in his preparation, he is readying us,
I feel, for the return of Christ! He is preparing us,
liberating us from fears and bondages, and giving us power
to be, and then power to do!

God is on the move!

In spite of the fact that he wants us to keep our eyes on
the message, and not on the messenger, we cannot ignore

the messenger. A feeling of awe surrounds me when I even think about God's goodness in bringing messages to his people by angelic beings.

As I look at an angel and hear him say that God cares about us, I realize it isn't just the angel who stands there. It is God himself who cares enough to bring this message to our hearts.

At times there are things which sound a little humorous in the ministry of angels and the work they do, but there is always a tremendous feeling of awe surrounding them because they come directly from the presence of God, and his glory comes with them.

If there had only been one visit, I would have been completely content because it is an experience of a lifetime. However, several weeks after the original encounter, the angels visited me for the second time, reinforcing the original message given to me. It didn't even stop there, and about five weeks later, just after I had gone to bed, I noticed a bluish glow coming from the staircase. I knew it was too dim to be the light for the staircase, so I thought that possibly I had left a light on in one of the downstairs rooms. I got up, and started down to turn the light off.

I was halfway down the stairs when the light flipped on! Standing before me were two of the largest men I had ever seen in my life! I was shocked! I wasn't exactly frightened, but there was such a radiation of divine power which comes from them dwelling in the brightness of God's presence, that I could not stand up! My knees buckled and I started to fall! One of these huge beings reached out, took hold of me, and my strength returned!

He very simply told me he was the angel Gabriel! I was stunned! Could this be the same Gabriel I had read about in the Bible? The impact of the first visits were far less awesome than now, because here he stood, as clearly visible as any earthly man, and introduced himself as the angel Gabriel! It is impossible to describe my feelings of awe and wonder! Then he introduced me to the second angel whose

name was Chrioni! CHRIONI? That's a peculiar name. I
never heard of that! Why not Mahalaleel, or Tubalcain, or
Shadrach, Meshach or Abednego, Asyncritus, Phlegon,
Philologus, Sosipater, or Onesiphorus? I had never thought
of all the angels having names, and as it turned out, all
having different appearances!

I asked Gabriel, "Why are the two of you here?" He
merely said that the Holy Spirit had sent them, and then
Gabriel immediately began telling me some beautiful truths.

Theologically, I knew that the Holy Spirit was everywhere at once, but it took on new meaning when he told
me that the Holy Spirit constantly monitors the whole
earth and picks up the signals from everywhere at once. He
even hears a bird as it falls to the ground, wherever it is!
He hears the softest footsteps, and he cares! "The Lord is
still in his holy temple; he still rules from heaven. *He
closely watches everything that happens here on earth"* (Ps.
11:4 TLB).

He said that in seeing what is happening throughout the
whole earth, he detected a massive build-up of satanic
forces who were planning to attack me. The Spirit not only
monitors, but sends out orders, so at God's command, the
angels were right here in Boise, Idaho, to defeat the enemy!

I was a little concerned because I didn't want them
standing around if the enemy was going to attack (I wanted
them to be out fighting!) but he said, "We have already
finished the job!"

I asked him if they normally come in answer to a call
for help.

"No," he replied, "if the Spirit waited until you knew
about an attack, you would already be in trouble! This is
not anything unusual. We are constantly holding back the
enemy and putting them to flight!"

Then he asked me to look out the window. I looked,
and there were about a hundred of these big warring angels
standing in the driveway. They had already finished their
job and were just casually talking with each other! It gave

me a real good feeling to know that God has ways and means of taking care of his people!

Gabriel spoke to me about the enormity of the spirit of iniquity which is working overtime in the world today. There is a sinister attempt by deceiving spirits to get God's people sidetracked from the living Christ. He wants to be a living, pulsating person to every one of us, but because of these enemy forces, some people have taken their eyes off of Jesus and started looking to teachers. Some of these teachers dissect and categorize the Bible until it loses its life. Gabriel said, "Read the Word, feed on it, let it become the Living Word to you, not just columns of truths and opinions of men." He referred to Christ being known as a blackboard Christ, a diagrammed Christ, a printed Christ, or even as a flannelgraph Christ. He said that Jesus wants to be known as the Living Christ, coming out the pages of the Bible to us! Hallelujah!

I felt this message was really needed! He added that though study sounds spiritual, some people would always be learning, and never doing, because by the time they acquired knowledge of one type of a study or doctrine, it was out-of-date and they had to start all over again! He said, "Feed on the Word." He repeated, "Feed on the Word!" Don't settle for the dissected Word torn into little bits and analyzed by sections. Keep it the Living Word! This is exciting because there is no substitute for Jesus WITH you and IN you!

He told me about different types of angels, such as praise angels, worship angels, ministering angels, and warring angels. Regardless of their function, their highest purpose is to exalt the name of Jesus! When that name sounds in heaven or here on earth, they fall face down and worship him because he is so exalted!

One night while Gabriel and Chrioni were talking to me, there suddenly appeared a bluish shaft of pure light about eighteen inches in diameter from the ceiling to the floor of our study room.

The instant the light appeared, both angels fell prostrate on the floor. They stayed in a prone position for at least five minutes without a single motion or sound. I didn't know what to do, so I fell on my hands and knees and worshipped God.

They never told me what this was, but I feel that just as a bright light appeared to Saul on the road to Damascus, this also could have been an appearance of Jesus in the form of a bright light. It was awesome to me!

Some of the unique experiences God has blessed me with are so unbelievable from our human viewpoint that I am often hesitant to share them publicly. Here is one of them:

During a visit one night, Gabriel said that God had sent me a little gift for my strength and energy as he handed me a round wafer approximately five inches in diameter and 5/8 inch thick, that looked like bread. He instructed me to eat it; so I did. It had the taste of honey. When I finished the bread, he gave me a silver-like ladle filled with what appeared to be water. I drank every drop of it, and an overwhelming desire to praise and worship God instantly came over me. Rivers of praise billowed up to God, bubbling up out of my innermost being, and for days after I drank this liquid, there was a sensation of "fizzing" inside of my veins. What an indescribably pleasant and exhilerating feeling it was!

The effects were astounding because the first day after I ate the wafer and drank the water, I LOST FIVE POUNDS!

The second day I LOST ANOTHER FIVE POUNDS!

The third and fourth days ANOTHER FIVE POUNDS EACH DAY.

Then it tapered off to about a pound a day. I had an excess of "flab," and that is all gone now. When I jogged prior to this, I quickly became winded, but now I have no breath shortage at all. My strength and stamina have been fantastic!

Praise God for his everlasting Word, the Bible, which is our stabilization point for all things, because there is a story in the Bible of the time when Elijah was weak from hunger, and God dispatched an angel to bring him something to eat. After that, he went for forty days and nights without food! God's Word is constantly being confirmed by the fulfilling of scriptures through activities on earth today not unlike those which have occurred throughout all of God's plan.

Another of the many beautiful truths God gave me through the mouth of the angel Gabriel was that everything God has promised is already completed as far as God's book in heaven is concerned. This statement was very difficult for me to understand, so Gabriel took a pencil which I held in my hand, and drew a rough sketch of a picture frame. Here is a photograph of the actual sketch he drew on a yellow pad as he explained it to me.

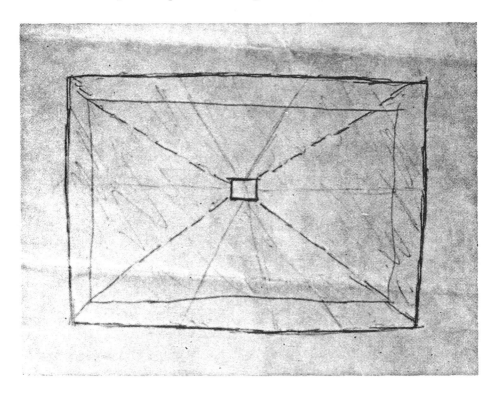

Everything God has promised is complete in this picture.
But, he said, "Here is a tiny little spot representing things
unclear to you – things not yet complete. You often spend
your time looking at these things until the tiny spot
expands outward and fills the frame, and totally hides what
God has done. If you look to Jesus instead of the problem,
you will see the complete picture."

In Is. 43:2 the Lord said, "When you go through deep
waters and great trouble, I will be with you." If you look
at the waters of trouble, it will hide the picture, but if you
look to Jesus, that little piece that looks so ominous to
you has to shrink back into place and then you will see the
whole picture complete with everything that God has
promised.

Many people have asked me if Gabriel had said anything
about the return of Christ. He hadn't, so I asked him if he
could tell me anything about it. He replied that Jesus is
returning, but the time is something that God has reserved
in his own knowledge. Gabriel has access to the timetable
on everything else that has been predicted, but God has
kept this particular secret to himself. Then he said to me,
"I can tell you this: there has never been such excitement
and activity in the courts of heaven since Jesus came the
first time as there is right now!" Hallelujah!

These angels spoke in a heavenly language and were
constantly picking up messages from the Spirit. Often when
they would pick up reports, they would laugh and become
extremely happy. Obviously, these were reports of great
victories that they were celebrating.

As Gabriel was talking with me, Chrioni, the other angel,
played with Queenie, tickling her ears, getting her on her
back and having fun with her. Queenie lapped it up! I wish
she could talk because I would like to know what her
impressions were. She has had a rare experience for a dog,
and acted as though she thought it was really great!

Gabriel went to the door and reached for the knob. He
said he had to leave because of an urgent call of the Spirit,

but he said, "I have asked Chrioni to stay here with you during this time while I am gone. I'll be back shortly."

It was so strange, because while I WAS LOOKING AT HIM, HE JUST VANISHED INTO THIN AIR. There was no flash, no sounds, no nothing. He just disappeared! One minute I was talking with a very solid, muscular individual, and the next instant there was nothing! All I could see was the place where he had been standing. He had completely vanished!

Everyone seems to be interested in knowing something about the physical appearance of angels. No two of them look alike! They are different sizes, have different hair styles, and completely different appearances. Chrioni has a hairdo much like many men have today, and he looks about twenty-five years old. I do not know what he would weigh in earthly pounds, but my guess would be close to 400 pounds. He is huge, seven or more feet in height, and often wears a brown pull-over shirt and is casually, but neatly dressed in loose-fitting brown trousers. His shirt laces at the top with what looks like a shoelace.

Gabriel often appears in a shimmering white tunic with a radiant gold belt about five inches wide, white trousers and highly polished, bronze-colored shoes. His hair is the color of gold!

The reason for the blue glow I had seen earlier was that their entire clothing was radiant, with an iridescent glow! Their skin also had a glow! And those eyes — I would recognize them anywhere! They were like balls of fire, but there was such warm compassion you could actually feel it in their gaze! It seemed as though they looked right through me! I understood what John meant when he described his meeting with Jesus in the first chapter of Revelation where he said his eyes were like "flames of fire."

There is something about being in the presence of God that creates a glow or shine. When Moses was with God for just forty days and forty nights, they had to put a veil over his face because it shone so much when he came down out of the mountain that they could not look at him! When Moses and Elijah came down to the mount directly from heaven and talked with Jesus, the disciples said they had "glistening" garments. They literally shone!

During one visit, Chrioni said that God had given him permission to answer questions which I might have. I was so overcome, I really didn't know what to ask him! I felt a tremendous awe, and yet there was great joy in his presence. I finally mustered up some courage and said, "I have often wondered what angels do in between the times of their known appearances. Three or four hundred years went by in the Bible without one word having been written about angels. How do you keep from getting bored?"

He looked very puzzled when I asked him this question. Then he answered with the deepest, richest voice I have ever heard, "Those appearances mentioned in the Bible were just the times when the Lord opened the eyes of people so they could see us. Because there are always people around for us to take care of, we are busy ALL the time." Angels are beings of eternity. Time means nothing to them! Age means nothing to them!

We talked about different subjects than those I had discussed with Gabriel, and these pertained mostly to their work. He told me about another responsibility angels have, and that is to take care of the wicked and ungodly people. He said, "You can never comprehend the depth of God's love because it is too great!" It is so amazing to see how people can curse and hate God and turn their backs on him, and yet God's arms keep reaching out because he loves them so much.

I asked Chrioni to tell me about some of his most interesting experiences. One of the most exciting happenings reminded me of how old he must be, since angels were created before the earth was formed. It concerned the time when he helped lead the children of Israel out of the land of Egypt. He said, "God gave us the right to punish the

Egyptians and to use any of God's weapons. We threw lightning bolts at them! We pulled the wheels off their carts!"

He didn't actually say it was fun, but he did say it was fixed in his mind because of the great deliverance of Israel when the sea was pushed back.

He told me of another interesting event when Israel was on a forced march. "The men of Gibeon hurriedly sent messengers to Joshua at Gilgal. 'Come and help your servants!' they demanded. 'Come quickly and save us! For all the kings of the Amorites who live in the hills are here with their armies.' So Joshua and the Israeli army left Gilgal and went to rescue Gibeon. 'Don't be afraid of them,' the Lord said to Joshua, 'for they are already defeated! I have given them to you to destroy. Not a single one of them will be able to stand up to you' " (Josh. 10:5-8 TLB).

God had decreed that Israel would have the victory, so they *had* to have the victory, but they were too tired to fight!

Chrioni said the angels had orders to *intervene*, but not to *interfere* with what God was doing in man's normal course of life.

They had a terrific experience when a group of the warring angels made huge ice balls and threw them down on top of the enemy forces! "And it came to pass, as they fled from before Israel, and were in the going down to Bethhoron, that the Lord cast down great stones from heaven upon them unto Azekah, and they died: they were more which died with hailstones than they whom the children of Israel slew with the sword" (Josh. 10:11).

Angelic beings are continually ministering to people in many ways in these present days. Many seeming coincidences are really angels on the job! We haven't fully realized God's use of heavenly hosts to get his job done because of our limited information concerning angels. God let Paul see the power of these forces, and also David, who spoke of the tremendous numbers of angels and the greatness of their power. Paul said every one of them is sent forth of God to minister for those who shall be heirs of salvation (Hebrews 1:14).

God certainly doesn't want us to worship angels, but he does want us to be aware of them and their importance in our lives today. They are not just stories in the Bible; they are living, active beings working for God in the unfolding of his mighty eternal plan.

Gabriel also told me that God said many people would "fantasize" and report, "I saw an angel here, I saw an angel there." He said this would be normal because of human imagination, and because of a sincere desire to witness what God is doing through angels, but, he continued, "There *will* be definite times when people's eyes will be opened and they *will* see real angels, not just figments of their imagination." He also said that God and the angelic forces were just as near to people who do not see them as to those who actually do!

I am glad the Lord has allowed me to live in such an exciting day! These are the best days of all history! Things might look dark in some areas, but when you project Jesus over them, they look light. He tells us, "The whole earth is filled with his glory!"

MY VISIT TO THE THRONE ROOM

The chain of strange happenings in my life dates back to January 21, 1977, when I became God's guest.

I discovered he wants to be treated like a friend. His words to me . . . "Relax, I already know you," have changed my life.

When he said, "I don't record failure," he opened a door of hope for all of mankind.

CHAPTER 4

MY VISIT TO THE THRONE ROOM

One Saturday night in January of 1977, at about 10:30 o'clock, I was seated at my desk, meditating, praying, and preparing my heart for Sunday. I had my head down on my arm at the desk, when suddenly, without any warning, I was taken right out of that room!

I heard a voice say: "Come with me into the Throne Room where the secrets of the universe are kept!" I didn't have time to answer; space means nothing to God! It was like a snap of the fingers — boom — and I was right there! Only then did I recognize that the voice I had heard speaking to me was the voice of the Almighty God!

I was nervous, and God told me to relax. He said, "You can't prove anything to me, because I already know you. I began to relax even though it was so awesome I had difficulty comprehending what was happening.

He came right to the point and said, "I want to give you (and this is HIS expression) an 'overlay' of truth." In a split second of eternity, we went from Genesis to Revelation, looking first at God's plan for his people. Throughout all of the Bible, God discussed his character, stating, I will do nothing in conflict with my nature or my character. My plan for you is good and it will be accomplished."

He referred me to Jeremiah 29:11, "For I know the thoughts that I think toward you, saith the Lord, thoughts of peace, and not of evil, to give you an expected end." In giving me these thoughts, God wanted me to see how he really felt about man; that he had man in mind before he made the earth; and he made the earth so man would have a place on which to live. When he looks at man, he does not look at the evil which has taken place, but he looks at the very heart of man.

During this visit, God truly gave me a glorious glimpse of the hidden secrets of the universe; of matter, energy, nature and space, all bearing the same beautiful trademark. As he gave me this dazzling overlay of truth, it added a new beauty and unity to the entire Bible which I previously did not have. Certain biblical truths which I had seen darkly were now perfectly clear, and I could see how all the pieces fit together in what God was doing!

Then God said I could ask questions! My mind was whirling! How does a human ask questions of God? It was so awesome being in his presence I could hardly think. Finally a thought came into my mind to find out whether or not he actually made individual plans for each and every life, because for some reason or other, I felt this gigantic task would be too big even for God!

In answer to my question, God let me see the vastness of his heavenly archives! My head swam! There was no way my finite mind could understand how God could keep track of these files. There must be billions of them! He said, "Since you are overwhelmed by this, and it staggers you, let me pull out one that you can relate to." And he immediately pulled out mine! He would not let me see the contents of it, but mentioned a few of the future items listed which I could use as confirmation of this visit.

Then he did another very surprising thing! He wrote down 120 events which he said would happen in my life in the future. It wasn't like you and I write; the information just suddenly appeared! I did not even need to read it, but right now, I can tell you EVERYTHING that was on that paper, because it was instantly impressed on my mind like a printing press prints on paper. The press doesn't have to read what is imprinted. It's there! In the same way, every single notation was burned into my mind, and it's still there!

Even though I had this knowledge, God also let me know that he did not want me to reveal any of these things until such time as he would release me to share them.

He said, "Let me show you someone else's record that you will easily understand." He pulled out the file on Cyrus and reminded me of the last verse of Isaiah 44, and the first five verses of 45 where he said, "When I say of Cyrus, 'He is my shepherd,' he will certainly do as I say; and Jerusalem will be rebuilt and the Temple restored, for I have spoken it.

"This is Jehovah's message to Cyrus, God's anointed, whom he has chosen to conquer many lands. God shall empower his right hand and he shall crush the strength of mighty kings. God shall open the gates of Babylon to him; the gates shall not be shut against him any more. I will go before you, Cyrus, and level the mountains and smash down the city gates of brass and iron bars. And I will give you treasures hidden in the darkness, secret riches; and you will know that I am doing this — I, the Lord, the God of Israel, the one who calls you by your name.

"And why have I named you for this work? For the sake of Jacob, my servant — Israel, my chosen. I called you by name *when you didn't know me"* (TLB). God looked far into the future and saw exactly what was going to happen.

He allowed me to see the record books, and also his blueprints for many lives. One book was that of the apostle Paul. It revealed that he would be used to bring the gospel to kings, rulers, and men of authority. For this reason, God gave him a bigger brain capacity than normal, and because he was more brilliant, he caused him to study under the greatest teachers of his day, finally being tutored by Gamaliel, the most outstanding teacher of that time. God had chosen Paul to write the scripture, the epistles, his plan for the church and his body, so he prepared him for this task.

One of the most exciting things to me was the peek that

God gave me into Abraham's and Sarah's records. As I glanced through them, I saw things with which I was totally unfamiliar. I saw records of Abraham's and Sarah's hospitality to strangers. They had a real feeling for those who were less fortunate than they. They watered the camels of their guests, gave them a place to stay, and shared their food with them. God honored this, and it was written down, but I had never previously noticed this when I read the book of Genesis!

One thing I could not find was the places where Abraham stumbled. When Abraham lied to the king of Egypt, saying that his wife was his sister, it was not recorded there! The time his faith was weak and he laughed because of unbelief in God's promise that a man of his age could be a father, was not recorded there.

"God, where is the other book?"

"I have no other book for the believers."

"Where did you write about the failures of Abraham which I have seen recorded in your own words in the Bible?"

"I have no other book. I DO NOT RECORD FAILURE IN HEAVEN!" (See Heb. 10:17-18.)

This is a beautiful hope for all of mankind!

Eternity files are not like man would make; they are more complete, and everything is meticulously recorded. These are the records he will bring into focus when the books are opened at the believers' judgment. This is the heavenly filing system, a totally different dimension than that of this world; an eternity of archives.

Another of the exciting things God did was to take me in spirit to visit the homes of several families in my church. Without seemingly any expenditure of time, God took me from one home to another, just like we were going from door to door. As we listened to the conversations of people in these homes, it seemed strange to be in the room with people talking who apparently didn't know I was there. I could see them, but it appeared as though they were looking right through me. Then I thought about the fact that Christ is in homes, listening, watching what is going on, and often we are totally unaware that he is there!

There were countless angels everywhere. For a fleeting period of time I saw my own church building packed with angels. There were more heavenly beings than earthly beings! Hallelujah!

There isn't any way I can tell you all the things that were imprinted on my mind during this time of unadulterated glory. It is utterly impossible! I do, however, want to share some of the things which made the greatest impression upon me.

One of the discoveries which was so beautiful to me in heaven, was the total absence of the piety people often want to apply to their lives when they think of God! There was none there! Everything was on a light, happy, relaxed basis, with real brightness! I didn't feel like I had to walk on eggs because I was totally at ease! I didn't have to think twice of what I was going to say for fear I would displease someone for there was a sense of total openness. It was a beautiful, but awesome experience that I will never forget!

God emphasized to me that we should quit worrying about HIS responsibilities. He actually let me view people who are trying to serve him by seeing how much they can get their minds in tune with him, by trying to think just exactly right, or trying to say the right word at the right time! God emphasized to me, "That is my business. You worship me, walk with me, put your hand in mine, get your heart in tune with me and I will give you the privilege of moving with me.

"Let me take care of my own business! What I have promised is my business, and I will take care of it. I have not failed in all of this time. Not even one of my words has failed in all of my good promises."

I learned some things that were truly astounding! One of these was the fact that God let me know money isn't going to have a whole lot of value except when it is used for his

work. To those who direct their resources for his work, he
will open the channel wide and there will be no limit as to
how much he will bless them. He even let me see those
inside of my own church whom he was going to bless in a
financial way. These were people who did not have great
finances at the time, but because they felt the most
important thing in the world was to use their talents to
create a cash flow for the things of God, he told me he was
going to pour out blessings upon them.

Since that time I have taken a little peek at some of the
giving records. This is something I do not usually do, but I
wanted to see for myself if God had already blessed these
people. ALL OF THEM THAT THE LORD REFERRED
TO moved from a spot of meagerness in their giving to an
overwhelming amount!

Another of the extremely interesting things God told me
when I was with him was about outer space. God spoke of
the graveyards of stars in outer space. I talked to my wife
about it, and she was as amazed as I was.

There has been a lot of speculation about the empty
spaces in heaven. He explained that the reason it appears
that there are dark, empty spaces, is that the gravitational
pull of stars inside of themselves is so strong that it bends
their light rays back inside, so the stars go out and
consequently they do not give out light rays any more. The
black holes do not mean that there are no stars there, but
simply that their light has gone out and they cannot be
seen. The black holes are the graveyards of stars. God said
that when our thoughts turn inward, we become just like
the stars that are wandering in darkness.

A space engineer stopped by our house one night (July,
1978), and I discussed this with him. As I told him what
God had said to me about the stars going out, he was
astonished. He said, "I can't believe this! It is so amazing
that you are this knowledgeable about these matters as
most ministers do not know that there really are stars

which have gone out in these black holes." He said that this was not yet known by the public. My wife, Charm, smiled when he said that, because I had talked to her about this months before.

Later on he wrote me a letter saying,

> I was particularly amazed when you told me about outer space. I was really surprised when you explained how the Lord compared some people who formerly were Christians who lived and witnessed for the Lord, with some stars in the heavens which used to shine. Not only have these stars ceased to shine, they don't even reflect light which does come their way.

> To me, these are the "black holes" of outer space. You knew about scientific matters concerning things which most ministers are not knowledgeable. The Lord had to have given you this information.

God also reminded me that the earth is a wonderful place, because the whole earth is filled with his glory! He let me see an increasing number of people turning to him. Not people backing away, not a surrendering of the church, not a church heading underground, but a church triumphant!

I became totally relaxed and at ease with God. You don't have to "put your best foot forward," because he even knows what your worst foot looks like! There is no use putting on an act or trying to make an impression — just be yourself! I found it would be impossible to be any other way in heaven!

It seemed as though I was with the Lord for several months, possibly even longer. All the things I saw could fill a huge book of several hundred pages, but there is something about the dimension of eternity that you can't quite identify with time. I wouldn't have even had time to read the paper God showed me because it was less than five minutes from the time I left my office until I returned.

Eternity is not run by watches because time is not measured. Time is just for this earth. Eternity is not going to be a long, drawn-out existence. It is not some long, boring extension of time. It is not time at all! It is just a glorious experience of being!

When I began sharing these supernatural experiences with my church, I was a little leery about telling them because there could be many who would feel I had some "screws loose!" In the beginning there were times when I wondered myself if I had been having hallucinations. Just about the time I began to feel that way, God would cause things to happen exactly as he had written them on the paper!

When your time comes to leave this earth, don't worry about it, because heaven is not a drag! If things get bad here, don't worry about that either. God wants us to make the most of our lives while we are on his beautiful earth, to live for him, and be happy! God is not nearly as concerned as we are about a lot of things that people have put their little red flags on. What he asks is that we walk with him and love him. He wants us to look at what he is doing, because the grace of God and his glory fills the whole earth!

God also allowed me to see loved ones who had died. Then he let me see believers who were passing from this life. I saw their families in heaven being alerted by the angels that a loved one was coming home and for them to ready themselves to welcome them. Paul referred to these people as having "heavenly" or "celestial" bodies. This amplified and clarified for me another eternal dimension. They were identifiable, and appeared exactly the way they looked here, minus the cares, the hurts and other problems. They were constantly experiencing tremendous joy, excitement and happiness, for heaven is a place of continual discovery about the beauty of God!

God let me see something else I had never understood. There is an area between our permanent abiding place in heaven and this earth from which we can be brought back.

People who have died and have been restored to life at God's prerogative, were still in this area. They had not yet reached the place of their final abode. This does not say people have a second choice, but that God can return them to life if *he* chooses. I know this area is there because I saw it! I was there!

One thing God told me was so opposite to my theology that it was hard for me to adjust my understanding to the actual facts. I have preached that once you quit breathing, if you are not saved, and do not know God, you have missed heaven. God said that was not necessarily so. He said that there is a spot where the spirit of mankind may linger for a little time before going on to their permanent abode. Many people who have been clinically dead know they have had this experience. Some of them have approached the gates of hell, have even looked in, or have been able to look into heaven, and yet have come back. He did not try to give it in a textbook fashion so you could prove it, or teach it as a subject, but just as a fact! I remarked to God that this was totally against my theology, and he simply stated that he wasn't trying to compare it to my theology!

I saw a type of hallway, which was something like a corridor or a tunnel between life and death, a waiting room from which individuals enter into the final dwelling place. God told me that a person who dies and comes back has returned from this corridor.

I was totally at ease the entire time I was in the Throne Room, but it was all over too quickly. Suddenly I came back into my office, and saw myself with my head on my desk where I had been praying. Until that very instant, I thought I was in the Throne Room in my body, but I was not!

The Lord has a wonderful sense of humor, and there is a lot of laughter and joy in heaven. I could see the back of my head, and I remarked, "Lord, I certainly did not know the back of my head was getting that white!"

I was really shocked after I found myself back in my chair, because I STILL HAD THE PAPER THAT GOD HAD GIVEN ME! I didn't know what to do with it, but there it was, right in my hand. I knew he didn't want me to share it at that time, and it completely unnerved me. I carefully laid it on top of some other papers on my desk so nothing would happen to it and went home. My wife asked me why I was so pale and quiet. I told her exactly what had happened, and we talked about my visit to the Throne Room for a long time. We finally went to bed, and I got up early Sunday morning and went to my office for another look at the paper. I discovered IT HAD TURNED TO ASHES!

The ashes looked almost like fur. They were feathery light, sort of fuzzy looking, and the slightest breath caused them to move in a lacy manner! They reminded me of snowflakes, only they were a different color.

I didn't know what to do with them. I couldn't bring myself to throw them out, and I was afraid to move them, so I left them there until late in the day. Many people came into my office to look at them. I finally scooped them into an envelope, and this condensed them so they weren't the same consistency. I still have the envelope as a reminder of a calendar of events that I didn't put together. I personally do not have a thing to do with seeing that these events come to pass. God just let me see what he is doing, greatly increasing my faith! If God wasn't in it, I wouldn't know how to account for that paper and for those ashes. Many people heard about this and came from great distances to see the ashes which were very unusual. Several pastors saw them evaporate right off of their hands as they held them. In two-and-a-half weeks there was not even one speck of dust left!

Many have asked what the paper looked like. It was about as thick as a piece of leather, but white, slightly opaque. It appeared to have been torn on four sides, rather than cut, and it slightly resembled parchment.

Someone asked me if it seemed empty coming back to temporal things, but it doesn't, because it is all a part of his systematic plan for his eternal kingdom. I feel God is just as close here as there!

One of the most tremendous things that happened to me while I was there was when God mentioned that the Bible's highest purpose was to reveal his character. He gave me Jer. 9:23-24: "Thus saith the Lord, Let not the wise man glory in his wisdom, neither let the mighty man glory in his might, let not the rich man glory in his riches: But let him that glorieth glory in this, that he understandeth and knoweth me, that I am the Lord which exercise loving kindness, judgment, and righteousness, in the earth: for in these things I delight, saith the Lord."

Then he referred me to Exodus 34:6-7 where he told Moses, you can't see me, but I will tell you of myself, what I am like. "The Lord God, merciful and gracious, long-suffering, and abundant in goodness and truth, keeping mercy for thousands, forgiving iniquity and transgression and sin . . ." and then he went on to say, "Then for those who reject, there is the other side."

God gave me special illumination in over 2,000 verses of the Bible. Instantly I knew these verses and their scriptural references by memory. I have no way to explain how it was done! I don't need to recall them — it's like seeing them any time I desire.

It may seem strange to you, but the thought never occurred to me to see what God looked like. I was only aware of the brilliance of his radiant glory. Like Paul of old said, the wonders and the glories of that place find no adequate description in earthly languages.

SEQUEL TO THE THRONE ROOM

Would you say:

. . . Thirty correct predictions out of one hundred is phenomenal?

. . . How about 120 out of 120?

. . . God never misses. That is why you can rely wholly on him.

. . . God told me the pope has no more influence with him than the least of his saints, and has no greater privileges, but because his influence with man is great, his choice is God's concern. Therefore, in order to help in the restoration of his fragmented body, God had chosen a man named Karol Wojtyla of Poland.
Date of prediction: January 21, 1977
Date of fulfillment: October 16, 1978, Pope John Paul II.

CHAPTER 5

SEQUEL TO THE THRONE ROOM

One by one, the 120 events on the special list God had given to me while I was in his Throne Room, began to take place in the exact order listed! God had told me that these were markers along the road in confirmation of my visit to the Throne Room!

While I was there, God took me in a vision to my own office on earth, and let me see a lady who had been involved in witchcraft. He didn't tell me her name, but in one split second I saw this woman clearly and distinctly and noticed all the details of her appearance. In the vision, God told me to bind the spirits, cast them out, and set her free, and I did just that!

The following Tuesday night, a woman came into my office dressed exactly as God had shown her to me, and she was completely set free just as I had seen her in the vision in heaven. This was item number one on the list.

While I was in heaven, the Lord also let me see myself ministering in a place of real need. I didn't see the congregation as such, but I saw people who had various types of spiritual and physical bondages, and the Lord was beautifully giving them new life and victory. The name of the place was Christian Life Center, but it definitely wasn't our church.

On the following Monday, we received a telephone call from a pastor of a church in a very small town in Washington. God had placed it on his heart to call me and have me minister in his church. He didn't know why, but he KNEW that he had to call me. We checked the calendar and my wife called him back with some definite dates. When he answered the telephone she was amazed to hear these words, "Christian Life Center!" There it was, just like God had shown me! That was item number two.

One of the reasons I get excited about this is that when God says something, we don't have to follow him around and keep reminding him, nudging him, and saying, "God, I have to keep an eye on you to make sure that you do the things you said you would." God had to remind me several times, "You tend to your business, and I'll tend to mine." He jogged my memory over and over again as he repeated these same words! If he doesn't do what he said he would, there isn't anything I can do about it, but I know he will. I trust him, and he has never failed! If he doesn't do it today, he probably has it on his schedule for tomorrow. But he will do it! You don't ever have to worry about that!

Event number four on the list related to a man who was to accept Christ on February 4, 1977, and who would die on May 30 in an airplane crash! God saved him on the exact day he said he would!

He was in our services on the Friday before he died, and asked to have lunch with me, saying, "There are some things I just have to talk to you about." As we ate together he said, "Pastor, I have a strange feeling that I might be going to die. Will you tell me everything you can about heaven?"

I had to bite my lip because I KNEW what was going to happen, but couldn't tell him. God had said I could not because of the impact it would have on other lives! However, I did tell him everything I could about heaven!

Just exactly as God had said over four months before, he went to be with the Lord on May 30, 1977, when he was killed in an airplane crash!

Another exciting event, number 34, concerns a young man who had sold out his life to Satan as a satanic priest. The Lord had given me his name and had even let me see him. On God's designated date, he came into the church and I recognized him, greeted him, and told him to come back into my office. God saved him, blotted out all of the old evil that was in him, and gave him new hope and new victory!

Here is a letter I recently received from him:

As I related my life to you on April 9, 1977, you didn't seem surprised at anything I said. It was as if you already knew! I discovered later that you did because my name was on a list you had received from the Throne Room of the Almighty God. You had been expecting me, and it was no surprise to you that I accepted Jesus as my Lord and Savior.

My life had been a series of ups and downs. I was raised in a parsonage and had been to the altar many times, but somehow I never completely surrendered. I wandered from place to place, unsettled, undisciplined, with no purpose to my life, finally ending up in a spiritualist center. I became a medium and minister, holding seances and giving readings. Controlled by demons, I had sunk as low as a man can go. Truly "my house was left unto me desolate" (Matt. 23:38).

As I tried to break away from this way of life, my home became infested with rats that would not be killed! I lost my home, my dignity, and then my family. I had no place to go. I called my mom and dad in Idaho, and found that they still loved me. I left the spiritualist center and came to Idaho, and like the prodigal son, I was welcomed home! In a short time the Lord gave my family back to me and my wife and I took a trip to Hawaii. We met a couple there from Boise who invited us to your church. PRAISE THE LORD!

There is a white flag that stands in my office.
It reads: "I HAVE SURRENDERED!"

/s/ Jim Olson

Item number 63 was another one which God actually allowed me to see and witness in detail before it happened. It concerned a family who were having serious marital problems. While I was in heaven, I saw them coming into my office and noticed the date was on the paper when this was to occur.

When the date arrived, these particular people didn't show up. I wondered what had happened, so I decided to stay a little while longer at my office. A short time after my normal closing hour, the telephone rang and a person who didn't identify himself, said, "Pastor Buck, will you be in your office for a little while?"

I said, "Yes."

He didn't tell me who he was.

When they came to the door, I greeted them BY NAME! This really shook them up! Then I asked, "What brought you here?" They said they had been having terrible marital problems and decided they would have to go someplace to clear the air. They didn't know why, but they had decided to come to Boise, Idaho.

"We drove up here, rented a motel room, and when we got inside the room, we noticed the telephone book was lying open to the spot where you have your ad which reads, 'Counseling by appointment.' "

Instantly I knew that one of those angels had been there ahead of time and had opened the directory to the right place, and had also arranged at the front desk for them to get the right room.

As we conversed, the lady said, "We have had a good time driving up here together, things are all straightened out, and everything is going to be all right, so we won't waste your time. We'll be leaving now!"

I said, "No, you had better stay here, because that isn't the way it is." I told them that God had let me see this event happening months before. I said to the wife, "You have a gun in your purse, and you are planning to shoot your husband as soon as you get back to your motel."

He was really alarmed, and exclaimed, "You'd better not shoot me!" She was shaking all over.

I said, "Open your purse and give me that gun!"

She opened her purse and handed me the gun exactly as I had seen it happen before. Then her very soul cried out to God! She knew there was no way I could have known anything about the gun unless God had told me, and he had let me know about it almost six months before it happened!

Both of them immediately fell down on their faces before God. He washed their sins away and instantly put their marriage back together. I have had one beautiful letter from them since then. They are going to a good church in California, happy in the Lord and serving God!

God told me he wasn't listing everything that would happen. He said, "I just want to pick out a few things so you can see by confirmation that I am really on the job!" There were undoubtedly hundreds of happenings between each of these events, but he let me see just a few to have as markers along the road. People have asked me what is going to happen when all 120 events have come to pass. I would like to say that the future events are planned in advance, just as much as they were planned in the past, only I don't know about them, but you can rest assured God has everything all mapped out!

An interesting item on the list concerned a Jewish man who owns a great chain of restaurants. Through a beautiful set of circumstances he met and accepted Jesus as his Savior. Evidence of his experience was seen by his desire that the hundreds of employees in these restaurants across the country would have the same opportunity. He said, "Surely God cares as much about these employees as he does about me." When he told me who he was, my spirit leaped inside of me because his name was number 112!

Number 113 of the 120 events which God entered on this paper from my book in heaven on January 21, 1977, was the selection of a new pope. God told me the pope has no more influence with him than the least of his saints, and has no greater privileges, but because his influence with man is great, his choice is God's concern. Therefore, in order to help in the restoration of his fragmented body, God had chosen a man named Karol Wojtyla of Poland. This prophecy was fulfilled October 16, 1978, when he began his reign as Pope John Paul II.

Number 116 on the list had to do with Red China. God told me not to panic when diplomatic relations with Red China were restored, and Taiwan was seemingly cut off. God has not forgotten nor forsaken his people. God has chosen to open the doors so that through this small opening the bright rays of his light can shine, bringing light and deliverance from chains of darkness.

One of the things God told me when he brought me back from heaven was, "I will come to you again." How I love him! He has revisited me over and over again by means of these heavenly angelic beings with messages for today's world!

In answer to those who ask if angel beings will come at my call — this is not possible! They do not respond to human beings, because they don't take orders from anyone except God. I have heard many people say, "I command the angels to do this and that!" This is an effort in futility, because you can't command an angel to do one thing!

Every single order comes from God, and that is why I know when they are speaking they are echoing words right out of God's heart. This is why they don't listen to the objections of people when God orders them to minister to individuals.

"For since the messages from angels have always proved true and people have always been punished for disobeying them, what makes us think that we can escape if we are indifferent to this great salvation announced by the Lord

Jesus himself, and passed on to us by those who heard him speak?" (Heb. 2:2-3 TLB).

My visit to the Throne Room has changed my life completely! I know God in a more real and personal way than ever before. My times of prayer have become visits with him. The Bible took on a new dimension and began to live. It is apparent that this experience became a big part of my entire life for it has occupied almost all of my thoughts and meditations since it happened. Though I do not have the benefit of the heavenly paper since God turned it into ashes, every item written on it was burned into my mind like a photograph.

I have often mentally gone over the various items on the list wondering how God would bring them to pass. Some of the things looked like total impossibilities. Upon occasion I mused over these seemingly difficult prophecies, jotted down my thoughts, and dropped them into my files. Recently, for my personal enjoyment, I drew out some of these papers.

One was dated February 4, 1977, just two weeks after the Throne Room experience when most of the prophecies were still in the future. It read, "How can these things happen? He was saved today, but it also shows his death in an airplane accident, May 30, 1977, Memorial Day. I surely don't understand why."

As I think of the long list of events which have already been fulfilled, and these predictions that God said would definitely take place, I cannot help but thank him because he has kept his word. 117 of these great events, these prophecies by God, have been fulfilled in sequence. The other three are in the process of being fulfilled at the time of this writing.

The question is often asked if the number of events have any spiritual significance, and what their completion will mean. Actually, these 120 things are merely a minute fraction of God's unfolding plan. They are reference points along the way, reminding us of his faithfulness.

God placed in the Bible far more than 120 specific events which he predicted would happen. All those which were to happen up to this time have happened just exactly as he said they would, and those which are yet to come will surely come to pass. These miracles foretold are proof that he is God!

His unfolding plan will continue unabated, even though I may not have any more special markers along the way.

One of the greatest truths this message brings is the assurance that God has scheduled each day of our lives. As we walk with him, he will direct our path, and though unknown to us, he will bring to pass his purpose for each of us, just as surely as he has caused, or will cause, the 120 events to happen which were given to me that glorious day in the Throne Room.

GOD'S PRIORITIES

Queenie, that's my dog . . . a purebred
Great Dane . . . quietly "woofed" as she
pressed her wet nose against my face.
The time was 2 A.M. I knew what was
up by now. This is the way she rouses
me when she becomes aware that angelic
visitors are in the house.

Filled again with awe and wonder, I
listened as Gabriel stressed seven things
of utmost importance to God. Priorities
that the world must hear . . .

CHAPTER 6

GOD'S PRIORITIES

On a recent visit, Gabriel had me write down seven things he referred to as "God's Priorities." Seven is God's perfect number! I have reviewed these truths, fed on them, and mulled over them many times because they have been made so alive and real to me, and are in agreement with and supported completely by the Word of God.

FIRST PRIORITY: THE BLOOD OF JESUS

Every message the angel brought has pointed to the sacrifice of Jesus. His blood is important, because the demands of justice have been satisfied, the wrath of God appeased, and the records of iniquity erased through the shedding of that blood.

Why would God's wrath have to be appeased? He had to find an object to strike because the sin of this world violated his perfect righteousness. The shedding of the blood of Jesus diverted the stroke of God's hand from us, and Jesus paid the demands of God's judgment for our sins.

When Jesus went into heaven, he sprinkled his blood over all of the things which were there. The book which contained all of the records of our iniquities, our failings, and our faults, plus our inability to perform, was sprinkled.

The book of the old covenant listed God's demands, but in the new book he puts his laws into our hearts. It is no longer "Thou shalt not," but "I want to!" This beautiful truth Gabriel brought dealt with the perfect and complete sacrifice of Jesus, not our struggle with daily problems.

Many believers know that the record of the things between them and God is straightened out, but they worry about the things between man and man. Gabriel told me that God has even erased these from this book.

In the first covenant, he said he would remember all sin and iniquity. In the second covenant he said he would remember them no more because they have been blotted out by the blood of Jesus. He tasted death for every man and woman to liberate them from the bondage and penalty of sin (Heb. 2:9).

The blood of Jesus has been considered insignificant by many people. Some have even made the statement that the blood was of no more effect when spilled during the crucifixion than when it was flowing through his body in daily life; but God said that the blood of Jesus was so important that not one drop was wasted. It is the only blood that has ever been referred to as incorruptible. This was God's plan. In Hebrews 12:24, the writer states, "There it is, the blood that covered sin!" Forever throughout eternity, the blood has a place!

SECOND PRIORITY:
FELLOWSHIP AND COMMUNION WITH GOD

He wants us to be able to have rich and wonderful communion with him. He is accomplishing this through his Word and by his Spirit. God wants to fellowship with you! He wants you to enjoy an awareness of his presence every day!

God not only wants believers to come closer to him; he wants those who are far away from him to come, too. He said that if you would call to him from wherever you are, from the very farthest point in all creation, he would remove all the distance between you and him.

God WANTS you. He is not looking for reasons to disown you, but he is looking for reasons to help you and to bring you closer to himself. "Though your sins be as scarlet, they shall be as white as snow; though they be red like crimson, they shall be as wool" (Isa. 1:18).

THIRD PRIORITY: JESUS IS ALIVE

Jesus is alive! Death has been conquered!

Even though we may experience death as far as this physical life is concerned, this isn't the real death. The death of the soul, the real death, has been conquered!

When Christ tasted the second death, he actually experienced the judgment of God upon sin. He didn't taste physical death for us, because we still have to die, but he wants us to know that we don't have to worry about the second death because he has already taken care of that for all who are putting their trust in him.

The angel reminded me of how complete God's plan is, and gave the reference of Acts 2:24 where he referred to Jesus saying it was impossible for death to hold him. Why was it impossible? Because it was already recorded in heaven that he came out of death and hell. Because it was in God's plan, it was impossible that hell could hold him. Satan was defeated!

The beautiful story of what Jesus did is told in Hebrews 2:9-15 (TLB): "but we do see Jesus — who for awhile was a little lower than the angels — crowned now by God with glory and honor because he suffered death for us. Yes, because of God's great kindness, Jesus tasted death for everyone in all the world. And it was right and proper that God, who made everything for his own glory, should allow Jesus to suffer, for in doing this he was bringing vast multitudes of God's people to heaven; for his suffering made Jesus a perfect Leader, one fit to bring them into their salvation.

"We who have been made holy by Jesus, now have the same Father he has. That is why Jesus is not ashamed to call us his brothers. For he says in the book of Psalms, 'I will talk to my brothers about God my Father, and together we will sing his praises.' At another time he said, 'I will put my trust in God along with my brothers.' And at still another time, 'See, here am I and the children God gave me.'

"Since we, God's children, are human beings — made of flesh and blood — he became flesh and blood too by being born in human form; for only as a human being could he die and in dying break the power of the devil who had the power of death. Only in that way could he deliver those who through fear of death have been living all their lives as slaves to constant dread."

When the people who had put Jesus to death saw him living in those who belonged to him, instead of having only one Jesus to contend with, they had many! In fact, all of those who served him were reflecting his power and his life! The best way to let people know that he is alive today is to let them see you reflecting his life as he lives in you!

FOURTH PRIORITY:
THE PROMISE OF THE HOLY SPIRIT

God plans ahead! He didn't suddenly stumble upon the idea of giving power to his children! This great promise was planned before the earth was created, and we were informed of it in his prophecy, the Bible, long before the day of Pentecost arrived. It was a priority part of his total plan for the redemption of his people.

He wanted to make each and every one of us conformed to the image of his Son, so that as we view him (God), we are transformed into the same image from glory to glory! In order to do what Jesus did on earth, we must have the same power he had! In order to be like Jesus, we must have God's Holy Spirit!

There are many people today who rule this out, and there are some who say, "If it is true that an angel gave this message to you, he wouldn't be talking about the Holy Spirit because that is a controversial subject, and an angel would certainly stay on neutral ground." Gabriel didn't even comment as to whether or not it was controversial. He just stated a fact that this was high priority with God today!

FIFTH PRIORITY:
GO TELL THE WORLD

The fifth priority was enlarged upon one day when Gabriel was talking with me in my church office. He paced back and forth as he talked. It was the first time I had ever seen a severe look on his face. He said God was concerned that people would hear his message and be aroused to the truth, and then go back to sleep. One of the top priorities of God is that we GO TELL THE WORLD! Jesus said, go ye into all the world and carry this Good News:

God says, "You can come to me now!"

"The barriers are down!"

"You have been reconciled by the death of my Son!"

This is the message of redemption we are to carry to all the world! He has given us his plan. He has filled us with his Holy Spirit. He says, "Go ye." Now he has sent forth special forces of angels to move men toward God! It is important to God that people hear and know that he is not letting any stone go unturned.

One day Gabriel said that these heavenly beings were on every hill, every tree, and even in the holes of the ground, searching out men and women who are trying to hide from God! They are out there doing what we cannot do! We are so limited, but they are not. God is saying by this, "I want them to know I care, and I want them to come to me."

There are many who have their eyes on sin instead of God — constantly reminding others of the terrible condition of the world and the blackness of sin. That is not on God's priority list at all. He wants men to know that there is a total escape from that horrible bondage of sin. People already know how evil sin is. When they are bound and entangled by it, they certainly don't want to hear it from others. God said that he did not send his Son into the world to condemn the world, but to open the door of escape. He said his purpose is to make us "Son" conscious instead of "sin" conscious. He wants us to see Jesus lifted up so he can draw all men unto himself!

People have come to me who have had tremendous burdens on their heart and have felt the nudging, the drawing, the pulling of God's angels, as well as the Spirit of the Lord speaking to their heart. There was such a hunger for God that they have gone from church to church and instead of finding God, they have heard messages on how terrible things are. The wickedness of the world was pointed out to them, but they still left with an emptiness in their hearts and lives!

One man came into my office asking if there was help anywhere. He said, "This is the fifth church I have come to. I have to find God."

"You have come to the right spot here." I didn't even ask him what his sin was. I just said, "When you feel my hands on your head, I want you to say the name of Jesus just as loud as you can! He has been nudging you, he has been waiting for you to call." That man shouted one word, "JESUS!" and the Lord heard him and instantly life came into him!

SIXTH PRIORITY:
ATONEMENT OF JESUS IS EVERLASTING

People need to be reminded of this priority constantly. The work JESUS did for them IS AN EVERLASTING WORK! It isn't something that he did and then forgot about. It is something that is intended to help us, to carry us right through to heaven. It is the message of atonement, a message of new beginnings. Gabriel told me it was of high priority that people know and understand the sacrifice of Jesus, and that the blessings of atonement are a continuing thing. Every day that we live we can experience these blessings in our spirit, soul and body.

All of our needs are covered in the atonement. With his covering over us, God can see us and accept us. Without the atonement, Gabriel said, we could not be accepted. Because people are in bondage to fear, it is important to God that people know that before he made the earth, he planned that they would be covered by his atonement. This is why he said in Eph. 1:4: "Long ago, even before he made the world, God chose us to be his very own, through what Christ would do for us; he decided then to make us holy in his eyes, without a single fault — we who stand before him covered with his love" (TLB).

God talks about this in the twenty-fourth and twenty-fifth verse of Jude, "Now unto him that is able to keep you from falling, and to present you faultless before the presence of his glory with exceeding joy . . ." The atonement covers, cleanses, and removes the guilt. We cannot please God or really serve him if we are constantly living in fear that God has some hidden sin to bring against us. He wants us to know that our lives are covered when our faith and our trust are in him!

The reason this is of such high priority with God is that people cannot really serve him without genuine assurance that their position in him is safe. Knowing this is REAL security!

God is letting people know that he will not let them go without a struggle, but he also wants us to know that there ARE two things which will pull us out from under the covering. One is *rebellion* and the other is *idolatry*. Outside of that rebellious spirit and idolatry, the things which happen in the normal course of life will not separate you from the love of God, or from the beautiful protection of this covering. You can live for him in relaxed happiness, knowing that he is on the job! When angels speak, they cannot speak for themselves, but they are echoing a message from God's heart that he wants you to know you are safe!

SEVENTH PRIORITY:
THE RETURN OF JESUS

God is telling us to prepare ourselves for that great day! For those whose names are written in the Lamb's Book of Life, it will be glory! For those whose names are not there, it will be doom forever. The choice is ours today, and that choice is simply to choose to serve Jesus or to follow Satan into his eternal damnation.

Look at the contrasting results of our choices:

". . . suddenly two white-robed men (angels of God) were standing there among them, and said, 'Men of Galilee, why are you standing here staring at the sky? Jesus has gone away to heaven, and some day, just as he went, *he will return!*' " (Acts 1:10-11 TLB).

"And may the Lord make your love to grow and overflow to each other and to everyone else, just as our love does toward you. This will result in your hearts being made strong, sinless and holy by God our Father, so that you may stand before him guiltless *on that day when our Lord Jesus Christ returns with all those who belong to him*" (I Thes. 3:12-13 TLB).

"And I saw a great white throne and the one who sat upon it, from whose face the earth and sky fled away, but they found no place to hide. I saw the dead, great and small, standing before God; and The Books were opened, including the Book of Life. And the dead were judged according to the things written in The Books, each according to the deeds he had done. The oceans surrendered the bodies buried in them; and the earth and the underworld gave up the dead in them. Each was judged according to his deeds. And Death and Hell were thrown into the Lake of Fire. This is the Second Death — the Lake of Fire. And *if anyone's name was not found recorded in the Book of Life, he was thrown into the Lake of Fire"* (Rev. 20:11-15 TLB).

"In a vision he took me to a towering mountain peak and from there I watched that wondrous city, the holy Jerusalem, descending out of the skies from God. It was filled with the glory of God, and flashed and glowed like a precious gem, crystal clear like jasper" (Rev. 21:10-11 TLB).

"No temple could be seen in the city, for the Lord God Almighty and the Lamb are worshiped in it everywhere. And the city has no need of sun or moon to light it, for the glory of God and of the Lamb illuminate it. Its light will light the nations of the earth, and the rulers of the world will come and bring their glory to it. Its gates never close; they stay open all day long — and there is no night! And the glory and honor of all the nations shall be brought into it. Nothing evil will be permitted in it — no one immoral or dishonest — but *only those whose names are written in the Lamb's Book of Life"* (Rev. 21:22-27 TLB).

For those who choose him, the return of Jesus is the priority God is looking forward to with such excitement that the angels of heaven are rejoicing with him about it.

When Gabriel had finished telling me this message of God's top priorities, he said that they are so much a part of God's plan that he had them all spelled out even before he made the world.

He directed me to the twenty-third chapter of Leviticus, where God gave Moses plans for the tabernacle, a miniature model of his total plan. Then, to my amazement, he related every one of these priorities for us today, to the seven festivals God had given to Israel long ago!

I marvelled at God's recorded plans in the Old Testament which direct us to his plans for this day in which we live.

1. PRIORITY: THE BLOOD OF JESUS

FESTIVAL: THE PASSOVER OF THE LORD

This feast was a "type" of the death of Christ, his sacrifice, and the blood of Jesus that was so precious before God. It was written before God ever made the earth.

The bloodline of God and his family is the blood of Jesus, the thread of God's redemption story throughout the entire Bible, his plan! The delivery of the children of Israel was made possible when blood was sprinkled on the lintel and the side panels for a covering so that the destroyer would pass over the homes and not kill the firstborn of each family. Our great passover was provided when Jesus sprinkled his blood over the books in heaven to provide a covering for our sins so that we could be acceptable to God and be a part of his eternal family.

The first of God's priorities which Gabriel gave me was about the BLOOD OF JESUS, and the first on the list of the seven annual special days of the Lord was the PASSOVER OF THE LORD!

2. PRIORITY: FELLOWSHIP AND COMMUNION WITH GOD

FESTIVAL: THE FESTIVAL OF UNLEAVENED BREAD

This festival was to be celebrated beginning the day following the Passover. When Jesus provided deliverance from sin by his blood, God immediately provided a covering for our sins; not a condoning of sin, but a provision so we could be accepted by him.

Leaven is a type of sin, and at the festival they were to eat unleavened bread, representing sin pardoned. Under the new covenant, leavened bread was used because God provided justification. Instead of SIN, FAULT and FAILURE, God sees, through the covering he provided, HOLINESS,

BLAMELESSNESS and PERFECTION. Those who choose rebellion and idolatry voluntarily move out from under his covering. Those who choose obedience instead of rebellion voluntarily stay under his covering because they choose to love and serve God above self and above the desire to sin.

"For by that one offering he made forever perfect in the sight of God all those whom he is making holy.

"And the Holy Spirit testifies that this is so, for he has said, 'This is the agreement I will make with the people of Israel, though they broke their first agreement: I will write my laws into their minds so that they will always know my will, and I will put my laws in their hearts so that they will want to obey them.' And then he adds, 'I will never again remember their sins and lawless deeds' " (Heb. 10:14-17 TLB).

3. PRIORITY: JESUS IS ALIVE!

FESTIVAL: THE FESTIVAL OF FIRST FRUITS

Gabriel said this festival represents the resurrection of Jesus and his life. Not only is he alive, but it is already written down in God's book that we who are his will follow after him in the great resurrection. It's in God's big heart!

4. PRIORITY: THE PROMISE OF THE HOLY SPIRIT

FESTIVAL: THE FESTIVAL OF PENTECOST

The coming of the Holy Spirit at Pentecost is not something that was a little afterthought in God's mind. He had this all planned before he made the earth. The word "pentecost" simply means fifty. It was fifty days after the Passover. When he told the disciples to tarry in Jerusalem, it wasn't just a coincidence; it was God's plan unfolding, and exactly fifty days after the Passover, something new and powerful happened!

At the Feast of the Passover, they were as individual stalks of wheat before the Lord. When the disciples were all assembled together in one place in Jerusalem, they were individuals. There was no blend. It was not a church yet.

Concerning the feast of Pentecost, God was saying, "Take the grain, grind it into flour, and turn it into bread. Put some leaven in it because the church will never be without sin or evil in it." God has it covered, but on the underside of the covering where you live, sin often crops up.

He covers his church, even though sin (leaven) is present; by his Spirit and the power of the life-blood of Jesus, he cleanses it! By this he was saying, "I want you to grind the wheat and turn it into flour and make some loaves of bread. Make a strong unit which is called my body of believers, instead of having individual, separate believers. My body is going to come together by the power of the Holy Spirit. It's going to be blended as one. It is not, as some people think, a perfect body; so put the leaven in because it has to represent the church as it is."

I'm not excusing sin; I'm just glad that God made provision for us in spite of it, because his plan was to take care of ALL things.

In God's great plan, the baptism with the Holy Spirit is available for all his children and is necessary to help us to be and do!

God's Spirit must be in us, and it cannot be quenched; the flow of the Holy Spirit power must never be held back. "Do not quench (suppress or subdue) the (Holy) Spirit" (I Thes. 5:19 Amp).

The baptism with the Holy Spirit endues us with power to be like Jesus!

It is a vital part of God's plan. You cannot erase it! It's there! It is settled forever!

5. PRIORITY: GO TELL THE WORLD

FESTIVAL: THE FESTIVAL OF TRUMPETS

After the day of Pentecost was the Festival of the Trumpets where the people met to herald the sound, and we too have the message to herald the Good News. Let's get out where people don't know Jesus, be the voice of the trumpet, and carry the Good News that Jesus saves! His work is done!

The news is good! You can come now! Christ has defeated the devil! The battle is over, and we can go out with the trumpets! That is what he meant when he said, "... ye shall receive power, after that the Holy Ghost is come upon you: and ye shall be witnesses unto me both in Jerusalem, and in all Judaea, and in Samaria, and unto the uttermost part of the earth" (Acts 1:8).

6. PRIORITY: ATONEMENT OF JESUS
IS EVERLASTING
FESTIVAL: THE DAY OF ATONEMENT

The Festival of Atonement was a reminder that Israel's probation had expired and that their covering must be renewed. It was the time for the annual sacrifice for sin. It was a time when God reviewed all the charges against man each year and he stood hopeless and helpless before the all-seeing eye of God.

For this reason, man was given certain guidelines based on complete obedience so that he would earn a reprieve during this time of exposure. This annual offering for sin could never make people perfect, but would give them another year of probation (Lev. 23:27 and Lk. 1:8-12).

When we are born again and God's Holy Spirit gives us new life from heaven, our probation does not just expire, it is canceled; the covering is not just renewed, it is an everlasting covering through the sacrifice of Jesus.

What about those who sin, who remove themselves from under the covering of God's protection? Just as God provided a way under the old law, he has a way for them today — and that way is repentance and a return to fellowship since there is no other sacrifice, no other way!

"But if we confess our sins to him, he can be depended on to forgive us and to cleanse us from every wrong. (And it is perfectly proper for God to do this for us because Christ died to wash away our sins.)" (I John 1:9 TLB).

7. PRIORITY: THE RETURN OF JESUS

FESTIVAL: THE FESTIVAL OF TABERNACLES

The desire of God is that we live with him forever and forever. This festival was a totally joyous celebration. On the first day, the people were to build the shelters out of boughs of fruit trees laden with fruit, palm fronds, and the boughs of leafy trees, while rejoicing before the Lord their God. These were to be the shelters where God would dwell with them.

Long ago God said, "I want to take you where I am. I want to live with you by my Spirit, and then I want to take you to live with me forever." This wasn't something that happened or that was decided on by a committee of theologians. He told Moses to institute this feast, because "I want to tabernacle with you." You can't get away from the message of the return of Christ and God's taking us to live with him, because it is already established in heaven and it is going to unfold exactly the way God said it would!

We have the assurance that we are covered through God's grace and that he doesn't see our sin, our fault or failure, but sees us exactly like Jesus — holy, faultless and unreproveable (Col. 1:22). We can rest in his finished work. Our confidence in the completeness of his perfect plan will get others ready for that great day when he returns to receive us unto himself.

This is the last of the seven festivals given to Moses and this priority will bring to completion God's great plan of redemption.

These festivals were so important to God that he had Israel rehearse them every year as a symbol of leaving this world for the seven years of Tribulation judgment. Hallelujah!

HE TASTED DEATH

One time as the angels ministered to me, God allowed me to see Jesus as the sacrificed lamb . . . My heart broke . . . As this panorama of truth passed before me, I saw him as the lamb lying there in death.

. . . Then I saw the little lamb slowly start to rise, and as it rose up, it became a mighty ram with seven horns upon its head and it had seven eyes . . . "You have seen him die as the lamb, now see him as he arose the great conqueror, with complete power in heaven and earth given to him."

CHAPTER 7

HE TASTED DEATH

Early one morning the Holy Spirit said,

Write, preserve the words which I have spoken to you. They shall become a light to many. I will not only minister through you, but will accompany these words, and give them life wherever sent, even as I have already given wings to my messages brought to you by the angel of the Lord. Fear not to speak in his name, for the words I give are not your words, but his words, and are established forever. Are they not found in his eternal, living Word? Long closed doors of many peoples and nations will be penetrated by these words of life. I command the hosts of the Lord who have been sent forth for this hour to hasten the gathering together unto him a people for his name, and to prepare them for that great day of the Lord. They will both precede and follow these words from the Father to make ready the people, to scatter forces of darkness, and to gently care for the multitudes who will hear.

There are often mixed reactions in people's minds when we speak of the supernatural. There have been many different types of reaction to the visitation of angels, or some supernatural truth that God has brought, because it is a little jolt, but in most cases, skepticism quickly leaves when people listen to the messages themselves. Down in their hearts, people are sincerely hoping that God IS revisiting his people in a special way.

As the Lord has dealt with me since that morning, I have mused over these words he told me to write and preserve, and questioned, "What is the heart of his message? What is the truth that God is bringing to the world today? Is it something so important to God that he is using divine messengers to quicken the Word where people have failed to discern what he has really said?"

He is not giving us a new Word. He is taking his Word, the Bible, and turning a light on inside of it, making it alive!

That question ran over and over in my mind, "God, what is the heart of the message that you want the world to have at this hour?" As I think about all of the thrilling messages that the Lord has given to me through angels, I realize all of them point back to one central truth. This has proven to be the very heart of God, the heart of the Bible, the heart of all history. The very core, the very center of God's message to us is THE SACRIFICE OF JESUS!

Jesus came from the bosom of the Father. The Word tells us he was a lamb, slain before the foundation of the earth (Rev. 13:8). The sacrifice of Jesus was the very heart of God exposed to man. Everything that God has done gravitates around the completed work of Jesus and that instant when he hung on the cross and breathed those words, "IT IS FINISHED." The sacrifice of Jesus was the heart of God and the heart of his message!

Christ has become the heart of society and civilization. History must date to Christ from both sides. Wherever Christ and his message have been carried, there has been light. Where he has not gone or where the message has failed to penetrate, there is darkness. He is the center of life! He is the heart! Without Jesus, the very life, the very heartbeat would be gone from everything.

Oh God, may we never be the same because we will see, we will know, we will feel, we will have, we will live, because of what the death of Christ has brought to us. May this be the time in our lives when we take out the contract you made with us, written in the blood of Jesus, look at it, and recognize that something very special took place.

It was not merely the snuffing out of his life, and the putting to death of his human mortality! Thousands of people have suffered physical death and torment, but this was not the death he was referring to. The death he refers to was not just the stopping of his heart. It was not the cessation of his breath, it was not the end of life forces for him, and it was not only separation. It was more! We know the pangs of earthly death and we also know that death hurts because of separation from friends, loved ones and earthly activities, but his was not just a separation from things held dear.

God told Adam and Eve that the day they ate of the fruit was the day they were going to die, and the Word also tells us that the soul that sinneth, it shall die!

God's eyes are upon each person who has ever lived, whether they know Jesus or not! Even the ungodly are cared for by God! His arms are stretched out to people when they are still in their sins. God tells us that when we were his enemies, he loved us enough to give Christ to die for us, even before we knew him. This was not for the cessation of our life on earth. We will still have to taste the earthly death, or else be changed so that we can leave this mortality.

The second death which faces mankind brings fear, dread and torment to him all of his lifetime. This was the death Jesus took for us. When he hung there on the cross, it wasn't the anguish of the physical torment, although he felt everything that we could possibly feel; and it wasn't the separation from people whom he held dear, although he felt it just as keenly as anyone; but Jesus suffered pains that even the ungodly, those totally separated from God, had never felt, for the ungodly have never felt the pangs that come when the last little flicker of hope is extinguished and they hear the words, "Depart into eternal damnation."

While living on this earth, they have never felt the weight, the hopelessness and the horror of feeling the cold side of God as he turned his back on them. Jesus suffered the torment of a damned soul! From his heart he cried out, "Oh, God, why have you forsaken me?" and the cold pangs of eternal damnation, those icy fingers gripped his life, and Jesus suffered the judgment of God. He was totally separated from God at that moment!

Oh, God! Oh God! Oh God! Oh God! I want to bring this truth to people. Build a picture before us right now. Let us see what you have done. Let us see your love for us that was so great that your only begotten Son became our substitute!

The Spirit told me to give the message that your sin has already been judged; the separating barriers between God and man are down; you are free, liberated by his power; and you can be restored to a place of total innocence, to man's original position of closeness and fellowship with God.

The importance of this message is seen by the reminders of the sacrifice in every message that has been brought by the angel. I remember so distinctly the very first time Gabriel came, he unfolded a beautiful truth from the third chapter of Zechariah. He said, "You have been aware of the sacrifice of Christ as seen from the earth which is from man's viewpoint; now would you like to see what happened from God's viewpoint?"

Instantly, he allowed me to see Jesus, the spotless lamb of God, totally sinless, as a moving, living panorama, coming from the Father to the earth. Then Gabriel said, "Now look at him as he returns to heaven." Then I saw Jesus bowed down, with his priestly garments torn and splattered with mud, filthy with the rot and the stench of the world. He came with his shoulders bowed, into the presence of God. My heart broke when I saw that. I saw Jesus in a different light than I had ever seen him before. I saw him coming into heaven from the darkness of the pit of hell, bearing the sins of the whole world.

Then as Jesus stood there, bowed, with God's back turned towards him, Gabriel, the angel of the Lord, spoke in a loud voice and said, "Take those filthy garments from him, remove them to a place where they will never be found, and put on him now the new, kingly robes, the royal priestly robes." Then the angels who stood before him placed the robes over him and Gabriel said, "Take a crown and put it on his head." On that crown was the message that ascended before God: "Holiness to the Lord!" Count all of those people who follow me as holy. Accept them because of what I have done. There it was, written right across the crown. That's when Jesus became our King and our High Priest!

I had read the third chapter of Zechariah many times, but not until Gabriel reminded me did it occur to me that in the Greek language the name of Joshua is really the name Jesus. I had never before seen the truth of how Jesus returned to heaven. All of Zechariah 3 is quoted here so that you will see the prophecy fulfilled exactly as God allowed me to see it in this beautiful vision:

"Then the angel showed me (in my vision) Joshua (Jesus) the High Priest standing before the Angel of the Lord; and Satan was there too, at the Angel's right hand, accusing Joshua of many things. And the Lord said to Satan, 'I reject your accusations, Satan; yes, I, the Lord, for I have decided to be merciful to Jerusalem — I rebuke you. I have decreed mercy to Joshua and his nation; they are like a burning stick pulled out of the fire.'

"Joshua's clothing was filthy as he stood before the Angel of the Lord. Then the Angel said to the others standing there, 'Remove his filthy clothing.' And turning to Joshua he said, 'See, I have taken away your sins, and now I am giving you these fine new clothes.' Then I (Zechariah) said, 'Please, could he also have a clean turban on his head?' So they gave him one.

"Then the Angel of the Lord spoke very solemnly to Joshua and said, 'The Lord of Hosts declares: "If you will follow the paths I set for you and do all I tell you to, then I will put you in charge of my Temple, to keep it holy; and I will let you walk in and out of my presence with these angels. Listen to me, O Joshua the High Priest, and all you other priests, you are illustrations of the good things to come. Don't you see? — Joshua represents my servant The Branch whom I will send. He will be the Foundation Stone of the Temple that Joshua is standing beside, and I will engrave this inscription on it seven times: I WILL REMOVE THE SINS OF THIS LAND IN A SINGLE DAY. And after that," the Lord of Hosts declares, "you will all live in peace and prosperity and each of you will own a home of your own where you can invite your neighbors." ' " (TLB).

The angel then brought me to Isaiah 53 and made some truths so real that I can never forget them. Beginning with verse 3, "He is despised and rejected of men; a man of sorrows, and acquainted with grief: and we hid as it were our faces from him; he was despised, and we esteemed him not. Surely he hath borne our griefs, and carried our sorrows: yet we did esteem him stricken, smitten of God, and afflicted. But he was wounded for our transgressions, he was bruised for our iniquities: the chastisement of our peace was upon him: and with his stripes we are healed. All we like sheep have gone astray; we have turned every one to his own way; and the Lord hath laid on him the iniquity of us all." There are those filthy garments that were laid upon him. "He was oppressed, and he was afflicted, yet he opened not his mouth: he is brought as a lamb to the slaughter, and as a sheep before her shearers is dumb, so he openeth not his mouth. He was taken from prison and from judgment: and who shall declare his generation? For he was cut off out of the land of the living: for the transgression of my people was he stricken. And he made his grave with the wicked, and with the rich in his death; because he had done no violence, neither was any deceit in his mouth" (vs. 4-9).

In verses 10 and 11 are the words that came right from the heart of God and I pray that they will grip you as they did me. "Yet it pleased the Lord to bruise him; he hath put him to grief: when thou shalt make his soul an offering for sin . . ." God took that undying soul and allowed him to swallow, not just a little taste of death, but a taste for every man. His eternal soul was given as an offering for sin.

As Jesus was put to grief, as he was bruised, as his soul was made an offering for sin, the Bible says now look upon him, look at him, he is giving birth to a new race! He was in travail; his soul travailed. Verse 11 says: "He shall see the travail of his soul, and shall be satisifed." Verse 10 says, "he shall see his seed, he shall prolong his days, and the pleasure of the Lord shall prosper in his hand." In making his soul an offering for sin, Jesus made eternal redemption possible for everyone, for the whole world!

From the agonies of a damned soul was born the seed springing forth. "He shall see his seed." He saw the church spring up, and he's looking today at his seed, his offspring, his redeemed, his ransomed, his liberated, who have sprouted up from his death! When he looks down at you, he says, "I remember the travail upon my soul, and what I see satisfies me and I like it. You are a member of the family, you are redeemed, you are a child of God. You are a member of a new race. Not a Jewish race, not a Gentile race, but a member of that new race, a member of the heavenly kingdom, a heavenly race, a royal priesthood!"

His death was Jesus actually being struck by God's hand with the judgment for sin for the entire world! At this point, Jesus entered into a total separation from God, and God turned his back upon him because of sin!

This great messenger that God sent brought this truth home to me so forcefully that as I saw it, I lay in bed and wept! I couldn't help it — the bed shook because of my seeing the price that Jesus paid and what his sacrifice and our remembering it really represents.

There is a day coming for many, many people who refuse to identify with Jesus, not realizing that he has already tasted death for them; that he has already become their substitute in judgment. There is a day coming when men will hear those words again, "Depart from me, ye cursed, into everlasting fire . . ." (Matt. 25:41). They will feel the agony that Jesus experienced, but they don't have to. God and the hosts of heaven are working full time today to spare men and women the awfulness of that day.

Audibly, or just from your heart, say, "Jesus, thank you for tasting death for me. Thank you for destroying all evidence of sin that has been held against me, for removing the records." It's just that simple!

As this beautiful panorama of truth continued to pass before me, I saw Jesus as the lamb lying there in death. Then I saw the little lamb slowly start to rise, and as it rose up, it became a mighty ram with seven horns upon its head and it had seven eyes. The angel asked me, "Do you know what these horns stand for?" He explained to me that horns signified power, and that the divinity, the completeness of heaven, of divine things, was always associated with the number seven.

He said, "You have seen him die as the lamb, now see him as he arose the great conqueror, with complete power in heaven and in earth given to him. Then Gabriel pointed to Matthew 28:18, 20B, and said, "See him now with his disciples; hear what he says, 'All power is given unto me in heaven and in earth . . . Lo, I am with you alway.' "

The greatness of our king who has all power, was centered on his sacrifice. Gabriel pointed to the lamb, followed by the ram coming forth (Rev. 5:6). Then he said, "You will see the honor that is given to him," and he allowed me to witness angels as far as I could see in every direction bowing down before him, and they cried out that he was the King of Kings, and Lord of Lords, and that he was going to reign forever and ever. Nothing was ever going to stop him. He was the lamb that was slain, but now he is alive forever more. Hallelujah!

Then the angel spoke to me again about the body of Jesus that was prepared by God for the sacrifice. This becomes especially important as we see the purpose of this sinless body. Jesus became the bearer of the sins of others because he was sinless. He was smitten, not for his own sins, but for ours!

Daniel had an opportunity to look at this in Daniel 9:21-25 (TLB): "Gabriel, whom I had seen in the earlier vision, flew swiftly to me at the time of the evening sacrifice, and said to me, 'Daniel, I am here to help you understand God's plans. The moment you began praying, a command was given. I am here to tell you what it was, for God loves you very much. Listen, and try to understand the meaning of the vision that you saw!

" 'The Lord has commanded 490 years of further punishment upon Jerusalem and your people. Then at last they will learn to stay away from sin, and their guilt will be cleansed; then the kingdom of everlasting righteousness will begin, and the Most Holy Place (in the Temple) will be rededicated, as the prophets have declared. Now listen! It will be forty-nine years plus 434 years (483 years) from the time the command is given to rebuild Jerusalem, until the Anointed One comes! Jerusalem's streets and walls will be rebuilt despite the perilous times.' "

This same Gabriel who was in my home showing me these truths, was the one who was telling Daniel that they had 483 years until Jesus would come to make a sacrifice and restitution for sin, not for his sins, but for the sins of others. Gabriel told Daniel when he could start counting for those 483 years, and it all ties together beautifully. Gabriel saw to it that the timing of God's plan was perfect. He said when Cyrus gave the decree that Jerusalem would be built, the clock started ticking. Gabriel said his function is in the fulfilling of God's plan, and he was the angel God assigned to instigate the action.

Gabriel told me he was the angel spoken of in Zechariah 1:12-17 (TLB), "Upon hearing this, the Angel of the Lord prayed this prayer: 'O Lord of Hosts, for seventy years your anger has raged against Jerusalem and the cities of Judah. How long will it be until you again show mercy to them?'

"And the Lord answered the angel who stood beside me, speaking words of comfort and assurance.

"Then the angel said, 'Shout out this message from the Lord of Hosts: Don't you think I care about what has happened to Judah and Jerusalem? I am as jealous as a husband for his captive wife. I am very angry with the heathen nations sitting around at ease, for I was only a little displeased with my people, but the nations afflicted them far beyond my intentions. Therefore the Lord declares: I have returned to Jerusalem filled with mercy; my Temple will be rebuilt, says the Lord of Hosts, and so will all Jerusalem. Say it again: The Lord of Hosts declares that the cities of Israel will again overflow with prosperity, and the Lord will again comfort Jerusalem and bless her and live in her.' "

Another time he allowed me to see Jesus going into heaven with his blood, not as the sacrifice with filthy garments, but as the priest with the blood of the covenant. I could see him as he entered, as he took the blood and sprinkled it on the holy things of God. I had never understood it in this way, but the blood also had to be sprinkled Godward on the things in heaven (Hebrews 9:19-28). Jesus went into heaven with his own blood and sprinkled it over the altar as the final sacrifice, the final covering of our sins!

Hebrews 10:16-23 (TLB) states, " 'This is the agreement I will make with the people of Israel, though they broke their first agreement: I will write my laws into their minds so that they will always know my will, and I will put my laws in their hearts so that they will want to obey them.' And then he adds, 'I will never again remember their sins and lawless deeds.'

"Now, when sins have once been forever forgiven and forgotten, there is no need to offer more sacrifices to get rid of them. And so, dear brothers, now we may walk right into the very Holy of Holies where God is, because of the blood of Jesus. This is the fresh, new, life-giving way which Christ has opened up for us by tearing the curtain – his human body – to let us into the holy presence of God.

"And since this great High Priest of ours rules over God's household, let us go right in, to God himself, with true hearts fully trusting him to receive us, because we have been sprinkled with Christ's blood to make us clean, and because our bodies have been washed with pure water.

"Now we can look forward to the salvation God has promised us. There is no longer any room for doubt, and we can tell others that salvation is ours, for there is no question that he will do what he says."

In this panorama of truth that the Lord allowed me to see, he brought me back to look at the book several times because it was so important. Gabriel said that the book on which God had instructed blood to be sprinkled was the book concerning man's dealing with man. He called my attention to Exodus, chapters 21-23. The other laws had to do with man's dealing with God and, among other things, concerned man's attitudes.

God gave the covenant to Moses just before he went into the mountain to get the Ten Commandments, and said to Moses, "Write it in a book, and then read it to the children of Israel."

"Then Moses announced to the people all the laws and regulations God had given him; and the people answered in unison, 'We will obey them all' " (Ex. 24:3 TLB).

They wanted to obey these laws, but the things of their everyday life caused their good intentions to fade away. People today are just the same, allowing the problems and interests of this world to pull their minds and hearts away from God's blessings.

Then guilt comes their way and they say, "I know that God has forgiven these great big old sins that I have had, but it's these little things that give me trouble; my attitudes toward my family and the people I work with every day." They say, "I really want to live for God, and each day I put myself in God's care, but these little things bother me. I'm afraid, because I can't get the victory over them." The Lord allowed me to see Jesus, the high priest, sprinkling his blood over the top of the book so that those things are covered. They are complete; totally fulfilled in Jesus. God sees the blood, not our faults, and we are accepted!

I believe that many of the ills and frustrations of believers come because they do not see the fullness of what Jesus' body means. Because of the accusations of Satan, and because of daily reminders of sins, failure, and human weakness, we often forget what Jesus has done. We are so aware of these other things, that we must be reminded that God in his wisdom has provided a time and a way for this to be accomplished.

In taking communion, you remember the Lord's death until he comes! He tasted the second death. He felt the full blast of it. The Word tells us that he bore all of our sins in his own body on the tree. He asks us to look upon his body, to see our sins, and the sins of the world placed upon him by God. Every lie, every sin against ourselves and others, every murder, all adultery, all immorality, all dishonesty, all cheating, all rebellion, all idolatry, all enmity through witchcraft and satanism; yes, everything we could be charged with is laid on him. He has become the sin bearer. He has become sin, bearing the concentrated dregs of the rottenness of billions of people.

Visualize him as the bulwark against Satan's attacks. God says, "See him, discern him, because if you don't, you are often weak, you are sickly, and you are subject to the attacks, the let-down and the draining of your spiritual strength. See him, not as something of beauty, but as that sacrifice, with that rottenness upon him, with every

murder, every lie, every bit of immorality, every bit of
wickedness that could possibly exist, all the stench of
homosexuality that caused Sodom to be burned; everything
laid upon him there!" Then as you see him, God wants you
to see on that body, YOUR sin, YOUR weaknesses, YOUR
failings, EVERYTHING that you have been worried about!

They are there, but they don't have any strength! They
are only the ashes of sins that used to be. Just the
burned-out cinders! When you see this, sin loses its grip and
its power to hurt you. Your sins are nothing but ashes,
because the blazing stroke of God's wrath and judgment
fell on that body. With all the sins laid on him, and all of
God's goodness poured into us, we can stand before God,
knowing that sin has lost its power over us.

Then we can follow the blood as Jesus, our high priest,
carries it into the presence of God for us, and covers,
destroys, and totally blots out all sins. This is exactly what
his blood did when he covered us. It blotted out every
record against us so that God's unfolding plan for us could
be complete. That plan is to restore us to the place of total
innocence and fellowship with God which Adam and Eve
enjoyed in the garden before sin came.

In Hebrews 10:5, Jesus is talking about the work God
gave him to do; the work of becoming a sacrifice for sin,
and he said, "A body hast thou prepared for me." A little
further down, in verse twenty, he said that we can now
enter into that place of close fellowship through his flesh.

Gabriel reminded me that the tabernacle had to be
exactly as God instructed, and the sacrifices were to be
carried out in every detail, because they represented God's
plan of redemption for all mankind. This plan was a picture
of Jesus and his sacrifice. He explained to me some
interesting truths which made the sacrifice of Jesus even
more meaningful.

A brazen altar was the first thing inside the tabernacle,
and on this altar the sacrifices were to be made. The offer-
ings were to be burned to ashes, and the ashes then were

sprinkled on individuals who were to be accepted of God. All the sins of Israel were placed on the sacrifice. Then the sacrifice, being made sin, felt the searing heat so that when Israel came to be accepted, and the ashes were sprinkled along with the blood, God was saying to Israel, "You have given me your sins. I am giving them back to you now, and letting you see the empty shells, the ashes of something that has lost its power and its life. It is reduced to nothing because the fire of judgment has been diverted to a substitute, and your sins which were there on the body of that substitute, were destroyed!"

Gabriel began with Hebrews 9:13-14 as he talked to me more about the sacrifice and its meaning. "For if the blood of bulls and of goats, and the ashes of an heifer sprinkling the unclean, sanctifieth to the purifying of the flesh: How much more shall the blood of Christ, who through the eternal Spirit offered himself without spot to God, purge your conscience from dead works to serve the living God?"

This kind of sacrifice was effective in Israel in the purifying of a life so that people could say, "It is done, it is done! My sins that were placed there are nothing but ashes; sin shall not have dominion over me; it has lost its sting, and its power." If they obtained freedom for a whole year through animal sacrifices, how much more shall the blood of Christ and his sacrifice purge and permanently remove sin from our minds, our consciences, and our emotions?

Jesus literally tasted hell for us, his body being struck by the righteous judgment of God. When the enemy comes our way, we can say, "Those sins that you are trying to haunt me with are nothing but burned out cinders, and the power of sin has been canceled!" We can joyfully say, "His wrath has been diverted from me to Jesus, and my sins were judged when he was judged!"

Look at Jesus, the High Priest, carrying his blood as he enters the very tabernacle of God in the heavens where the records of sin are kept! Gabriel said, "See him as he splashes his blood on the book of broken laws and upon the altar of the broken commandments as a thick cloud blotting out forever the records of anything that is written in heaven that you could be charged with. As we see him doing that, we see him bringing to us a new covenant."

Hebrews 10:16,17 says: "This is the covenant that I will make with them after those days, saith the Lord, I will put my laws into their hearts, and in their minds will I write them; And their sins and iniquities will I remember no more."

He has turned sin into cinders. He has blotted out the records and given us a brand new covenant. Do you know why he did that? It is because he WANTS us! He is not looking for reasons to destroy us, but to save us.

See him as the spotless lamb of God prepared from the foundation of the world. See him as the sin bearer coming before God with filthy garments, stricken of God, sprinkling his blood in heaven, sprinkling the book of the covenant that is now fulfilled. All of man's possible failures are covered by the blood that speaks to God, and it says, "It is done!"

In Israel there was a remembrance of sin made year after year after year. Man was pardoned, but sin was remembered. My heart was so stirred when Gabriel spoke to me with such commanding tones and said, "When Jesus came, the need for pardon was removed, because pardon reminds God of the sin which has already been forgiven. He completely removed the records of the stain and guilt. The blood of Jesus speaks and says, 'Justified, restored to a place of total innocence because of Christ. We are returned to the place we occupied before sin ever entered the world.' "

In the Old Testament, pardon came because of faith in the sacrifice. But Gabriel said when Jesus came, he WAS the sacrifice that took all the sins away. "For this reason you are not pardoned in God's eyes. Since Jesus made the sacrifice, not one person has been pardoned. God wants no reminder of those sins as they were previously remembered year after year, but he tells us now that they are NEVER to be remembered again!"

Gabriel said, "That's why you will never find the message of pardon in the New Testament. There is no need for pardon: IT HAS BEEN DONE!"

YOU ARE COVERED
(ATONEMENT)

I sat glued to my chair . . . unable to move . . . The same divine radiance which glowed from Moses' face after forty days with God, multiplied a hundred times from an eternity in God's presence, streamed from Gabriel's being and literally engulfed me. . . His word and his touch brought back my strength.

I cried . . . and you, too, will cry as you discover the beauty of this message he brought directly from God's big heart!

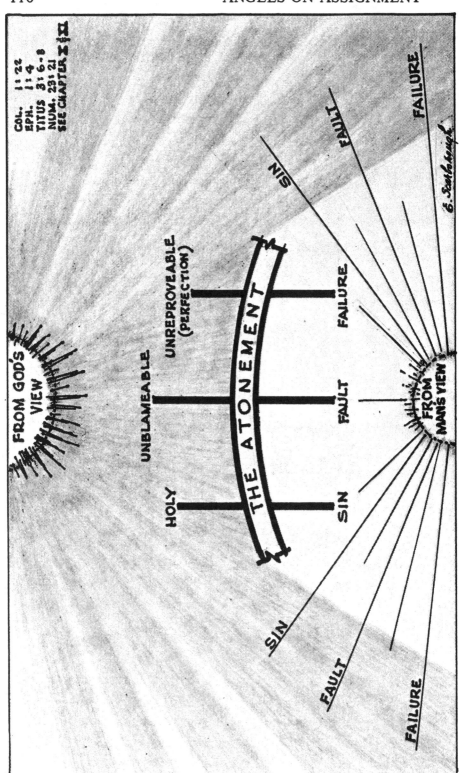

CHAPTER 8

YOU ARE COVERED
(ATONEMENT)

The message of atonement is a tremendously powerful and liberating message for Christians. It is a message that is included in God's unfolding plan for today and is for every person who lives on earth or who will live before the final day of the Lord arrives. Atonement actually means to cover (Heb. kaphar, to cover, cancel; Gr. katallage, exchange, reconciliation).

Gabriel showed me how to draw the diagram which explains the importance and function of the atonement.

This three-fold message is for those who are living for God, for those who are careless, and for the unbeliever, to let them know the awesomeness of God. This message is so important that it has been a part of every angelic visitation. It is the focal point of all history and for all people — it is the center of God's plan for the redemption of mankind. It is the launching pad for eternity.

The urgency and importance of this message is so significant that I feel challenged by God to tell you to get it into your heart, into your mind, and to talk about it with people wherever you are. Let people know what Jesus has done and what he can do.

In the center of the diagram is an arch, similar to a rainbow. This arch over us is the atonement, the covering, the blood of Christ. Above the atonement arch is God and the way he sees us. Below it is man and the way he sees us. Man sees us with sin, fault, and failure; but God looks through this covering, this atonement, and sees holiness instead of sin because he has already taken care of sin.

Instead of fault, God sees blamelessness. Instead of failures, he sees us unreproveable, he sees nothing with which we can be reproved, rebuked or even chided for (Col. 1:22 TLB).

God cannot tolerate sin because of his very nature. From his viewpoint, there must be total perfection before he can accept us. From our earthly viewpoint, we look for a way to make ourselves free from sin by pulling ourselves up by our own boot straps, but God explained holiness to me in an entirely new light.

Holiness is very similar to the glory of God. It is the outraying of his personality and his presence. Absence of sin is the *result* of *holiness,* not *holiness* itself. Holiness is literally the character and the nature of God.

GOD IS HOLY!

God speaks of the highway of holiness which reaches right down to earth. Through grace, God's unmerited favor, man approaches God on that highway. Jesus was and is the holiness of God extended to us, and he provides the way because he IS the way! We are accepted by God because Jesus was holy, and then we are covered with righteousness so that GOD SEES US EXACTLY LIKE HE SEES JESUS!

We see below the atonement arch (see diagram) the way we are viewed in the eyes of man. Man looks at our sin, our fault, and our failures from the underside, and accusations come against us both by people and by Satan. God's desire for us is that we see those about us as he sees them. To accomplish this, he has given us his Word, his Spirit, and the blood of his Son, Jesus!

Just as God cannot stand sin, he cannot even stand fault. When a lamb was sacrificed under the old law, not only did the lamb have to be perfect, without a single blemish or fault, but the priest who made the sacrifice had to be without blemish in order to function as a priest; he could not even have one mole on his entire body. God is a God of perfection!

God gave very strict and exact laws to Aaron, the high

priest, as to how he was to present sacrifices of animals for the atonement of the sins of God's chosen family, the children of Israel. God allowed me to see the Old Testament priest as he went in with the sacrifices to offer for the sins of the people, so they could be covered from one year to the next. I had previously interpreted this scripture to mean that the priest was ready to go into the holy place within the veil because he had done all the right things before he went in; that he had attained complete perfection by following every single one of God's instructions. I had always felt that this was sufficient preparation. But God let me see that this was not a complete understanding of the purpose of these rites.

Aaron, the high priest, and his successors, could only go to a certain place in the sacrifice before completing their preparation for entrance into the most holy place within the veil. It was called this because of the sacredness of this inner place of the tabernacle. The Ark, covered with the mercy seat, was kept behind the veil in the most holy place. God said, "For I myself am present in the cloud above the place of mercy." The one person in all the world who could have been spoken of as totally righteous, as totally ready, as totally prepared, would have been the high priest.

God allowed me to see this scene almost like a living panorama! I saw Aaron, the high priest, coming in, bringing a young bull, which had to be slain just for the cleansing of this priest. The blood of this calf had to be applied to Aaron and put on all of the articles in the room where he went. But he could not begin his work in the most holy place until something else happened!

He was instructed to take a handful of incense which had been beaten and pounded into a fine powder. This represented the scourging which Jesus had to endure for us. Then Aaron took some live coals directly from the fire, entered into the most holy place, and quickly put that handful of incense on the coals. Instantly a cloud billowed up from the incense and covered the mercy place above the Ark. Aaron became engulfed in the cloud which was a sweet-smelling incense that reached up and pleased God. Then when God looked down, he saw Aaron through the cloud which represented Jesus Christ and his suffering. Only by this act could Aaron save his own life.

Aaron's life was spared by a substitute sacrifice for the stroke of God's wrath. His hope of acceptance rested in what the incense represented, which was Jesus! Aaron was covered because the fire of judgment struck the substitute and Israel was given another year of reprieve.

Jesus, the sinless Son of God, went in as the high priest for the sins of the world with no atonement for himself. His hands were empty! He had no covering! God's wrath was diverted from man, and Jesus took the stroke of God's judgment upon himself!

A cloud arose from the burning incense which Jesus represented, that spread around the world. It moved back through history to the beginning of man. It moved ahead from Calvary to that great day of his coming! As it spread through time and space, it covered all people of all ages who have placed their trust in the eternal covering, God's sacrifice of Jesus!

After seeing the panorama of this beautiful truth, Gabriel told me that if I would like to read about this, I could find it in Leviticus 16:6, 11-12. Then he told me I could read about what happened to the people after Aaron offered the sacrifice. The blood of one of the goats (also a type of Jesus) which was the sacrifice for the sins of the people, was to be brought within the veil and sprinkled upon the place of mercy and in front of it. This covered the broken commandments which were man's sins, contained in the Ark of the Covenant.

After the rite of atonement was completed, the live goat was brought in. Aaron laid both hands upon the head of the live goat and confessed all the sins of the people over it. Then he sent the goat, with all these sins on it, into the desert where no one lived. This was the "scapegoat," and it took all the sins away. After first covering the sins of the people so he could accept them, then God totally removed all evidence of sin.

God wants us to know that when he covers our sin, he is not going to leave a rotting, smoldering pile of sin underneath the covering. He covers it first so he can accept us, then he takes it all away to a place where it can never be found. Our sins are not only covered, but they are removed as far as the east is from the west.

Because of the sacrifice of Jesus, which was the atonement for our sins, God can look down at us and upon all that happens in the normal course of this life, and our sins are hidden from him. That is his way of providing for our acceptance in the most holy place where he is present in the cloud above the place of mercy.

When God gave me this panoramic view of the atonement, or covering, Gabriel brought a message to me from God's heart, telling me that as Christians we can be completely relaxed in the glorious knowledge that he is taking excellent care of all things in his kingdom, and that believers do not need to feel weighted down once they understand their position in God. He told me that when God looks down upon us and sees our faith in Jesus and his sacrifice, he sees us looking just exactly like Jesus! We are accepted in the blood and wrapped up in his love. He referred me to Ephesians 1:4-5, and said God's intention was that man should be holy and without blame in his sight. "Long ago, even before he made the world, God chose us to be his very own, through what Christ would do for us; he decided then to make us *holy in his eyes, without a single fault* — we who stand before him covered with his love. (Eph. 1:4-5 TLB). Hallelujah!

God has given us his Word and his Holy Spirit because he wants the world to see us in the same way he sees us, which is looking like Jesus!

In Titus 2:11 it is written, "For the grace of God that bringeth salvation hath appeared (has been revealed) to all men." All men have not accepted salvation, but the provision has been made. It has a message of justification, of sinlessness, that beams up toward God; but it has a message that beams downward, "Teaching us that, denying ungodliness and worldly lusts, we should live soberly, righteously, and godly, in this present world" (Titus 2:12).

Then Gabriel reminded me that since we are now justified, we have already been accepted by God so these other things which are done by our own efforts and our own spiritual achievement are not for the purpose of God's acceptance, but so that men might see his likeness in us. "These things are good and profitable unto men" (Titus 3:8). They need to see Jesus in us, just like God does, then we actually become an extension of the beauty of Christ!

He gave me a reference in Colossians 1:21-22 where he said God has wrapped up this message in a brief verse just as he showed me on the atonement diagram. "And you, that were sometime alienated and enemies in your mind by wicked works, yet now hath he reconciled in the body of his flesh through death, to present you holy and unblameable and unreproveable IN HIS SIGHT:" Look back at the atonement diagram — from God's viewpoint. Then God lists the conditions for this to be so IN HIS SIGHT. Col. 1:23: "If ye continue in the FAITH (in his covering) grounded and settled (confident), and be not moved away from the HOPE OF THE GOSPEL (this Good news) . . ."

"For from the very beginning God decided that those who came to him — and all along he knew who would — should become like his Son, so that his Son would be the First, with many brothers. And having chosen us, he called us to come to him; and when we came he declared us 'not guilty,' filled us with Christ's goodness, gave us right standing with himself, and promised us his glory" (Romans 8:29-30 TLB).

He is saying that he will beam down on us the very

atmosphere of heaven and give us a little foretaste of what it is going to be like up there. This is the reason believers are happy. The Lord has literally given us a beautiful sampling of what he has in store for us because he has promised us his glory!

"Who dares accuse us whom God has chosen for his own? Will God? No! He is the one who has forgiven us and given us right standing with himself. Who then will condemn us? Will Christ? No! For he is the one who died for us and came back to life again for us and is sitting at the place of highest honor next to God, pleading for us there in heaven. Who then can ever keep Christ's love from us? When we have trouble or calamity, when we are hunted down or destroyed, is it because he doesn't love us anymore? And if we are hungry, or penniless, or in danger, or threatened with death, has God deserted us? No . . . but despite all this, overwhelming victory is ours through Christ who loves us enough to die for us" (Romans 8:33-37 TLB).

Because of his great love, God does not, and will not condemn us. Jesus said in his own words in John 3:16-17, "For God so loved the world, that he gave his only begotten Son, that whosoever believeth in him should not perish, but have everlasting life. For God sent not his Son into the world to condemn the world; but that the world through him might be saved."

Many people think Jesus came to condemn them, but the truth is, "He that believeth on him is not condemned: but he that believeth not is condemned already, because he hath not believed in the name of the only begotten Son of God" (John 3:18). God was saying in this scripture that this world had lost its way, and it needed a way out. His purpose in sending Jesus was to make a way for us to go into God's presence and remove the cloud of condemnation.

Great angels from heaven are around us to take charge of us and bear us up, lest we slip (See Psalm 91:11-12). God didn't save us to condemn us, but to give us life. His plan is to restore us into a place of fellowship and then reunite us with himself. This is God's plan! Hallelujah!

Because we are his, the atoning blood keeps on flowing to cleanse us all the time. We are not cleansed just by verbal confession, because our lips can say words we don't mean. Our true confession comes from the heart when our sincere desire is to please him. God loves us so much he wants us to know that we don't have to be on pins and needles in his presence, plagued by fear of failure in word, thought, or deed. When little things divert our attention, a little temper rises or a bad attitude creeps in, and we forget to ask God's forgiveness for it, he looks at our hearts and our intentions. We are justified under the new law because of what Jesus did when he died for us, and that precious blood continues to cleanse as long as we *want* to stay under the covering God provided, and he has also provided guiding signals from his Holy Spirit which are ever present to keep us under his covering.

In this day, the final message before the call of the trumpet for us to come higher, is the one of atonement. This follows the pattern which God gave in his plan of salvation before he made the earth. He wants people today to fully understand that they are covered, and the sinners need to know what God has in mind for them in order to enable them to come to him and be at peace with him.

Even if you refuse and reject him, nothing can separate you from his love. He loves even the most ungodly, but he does tell us in Exodus 34:7 that though his mercy and his loving kindness reaches out generation after generation, it will not clear the guilty; only faith in his sacrifice will do this. He loves people who are guilty and far away from him, and they are beginning to feel the warmth of his love. But this alone will not give you a ticket to heaven. It means that God loves you and gives you the opportunity to choose him, but the only provision for guilt is the acceptance of what Jesus has done.

We also need to remember that God is not only a God

of love, but he is also a God of wrath. Sometimes people are looking for a license or excuse to sin because they have no real desire to turn from evil. However, they still want to have the safety of the covering and are trying to pull it over themselves. God wants people to know that while he has provided a place of safety, there is also an edge beyond which the covering does not reach.

The things which give believers their biggest problems are not their sins against God, but the shortcomings and attitudes of man against man in their daily lives. "It is the thought-life that pollutes. For from within, out of men's hearts, come evil thoughts . . ." (Mark 7:20,21 TLB).

A shortcoming continued becomes sin, which is rebellion against God, and is not covered by the blood.

A shortcoming discontinued becomes obedience to God's wishes, and is covered by the blood. ". . . You can choose sin (with death) or else obedience (with acquittal) . . ." (Romans 6:16 TLB).

Moses and Aaron lived with the children of Israel and looking at them from earth level they saw evil in the camp. But from God's view from above the covering, God saw their obedience instead of their sin.

"He hath not beheld iniquity in Jacob, neither hath he seen perverseness in Israel: . . . (Num. 23:21). The Living Bible states, "He has not seen sin in Jacob."

God told Balaam he had looked at Israel from man's viewpoint, but now he wanted him to look at them through his eyes. In the 24th chapter of Numbers, Balaam said he saw something totally different now that his eyes were opened to see it the way God sees it. " 'He hath said, which heard the words of God, which saw the vision of the Almighty, falling into a trance, but having his eyes open: How goodly (not evil now) are thy tents, O Jacob and thy tabernacles, O Israel! As the valleys are they spread forth, as gardens by the river's side, as the trees of lign aloes which the Lord hath planted, and as cedar trees beside the waters.' "

God is not creating a big irrigation system so he can open the floodgates and water them all at the same time, but he is lovingly taking individual care of each one. He wants us to grow strong and healthy in him.

When the Lord spoke about this, I said, "God, what about Israel? If you had them so beautifully covered during this time, why did you punish them over and over and over again in between those sacrifices?"

God explained to me that rebellion and idolatry are the two things which will take man out from under the covering. It is not that God removes the covering, it is not that God goes down and looks under it, but man removes himself. Look at the life of Israel and you will find that whenever God smote them and punished them, it was because of rebellion or idolatry.

When people put their faith in anything other than what Jesus has done, they voluntarily choose to be out from under his protective covering. When this is their decision, they are exposed to God's eyes, and he sees their sins, faults, and failures.

Our sins were all washed away by the blood of the lamb, and the only way God looks at us is through the cleansing blood of Jesus. Then he sees:

Holiness instead of sin.

Blamelessness instead of fault.

Unreproveable (perfection) instead of failure.

We GET UNDER the covering by repenting of our sins.

We STAY UNDER the covering by wanting to please God, and by obeying him even to the thoughts and intents of our heart.

We GET OUT FROM UNDER the covering by rebellion or idolatry.

"AS FOR ME AND MY HOUSE, WE WILL SERVE THE LORD! (Josh. 24:19).

GOD'S WARNING SIGNALS

... It happened in broad daylight the
Saturday before Christmas ... The door
of my church office opened and once
again God's highest angel had come with
a special word from God ... Remember,
if you feel numb and cold inside and it's
a weight and a burden for you to think,
"Here's another week and I have to go
to church. I don't want to fail God,
but it's a chore; there is no excitement
in my spiritual life," WATCH OUT!

CHAPTER 9

GOD'S WARNING SIGNALS

God wants us to enjoy skating on his lake of joy while we are on this earth, but he also wants us to keep away from the area marked "THIN ICE!" This is simple to do, for he has clearly marked the warning signs in the Bible.

We don't have to worry and fret trying to live a Christian life. When we are walking with him in his light, we have complete freedom from fear and we never have to be afraid! His heart is beating twenty-four hours a day, and as long as it beats, which is for all of eternity, we are totally and completely protected while we are serving him.

God loves us so much that he offers us everything in heaven and earth, even making us joint-heirs with Jesus. However, some individuals still choose to voluntarily walk out from under the atonement (the covering, or the blood of Jesus) through REBELLION and IDOLATRY.

To rebel is to refuse allegiance to or resist the authority of someone or some authority over you. God is our authority. To rebel against him is to turn our backs on that which he offers: the protection, the blessings, the love and the promises. Throughout the Bible, God plainly spells out the overwhelming blessings which come when we submit to his absolute control, and the curses which come when we resist or rebel against him.

Idolatry is excessive attachment or veneration for some person or thing; admiration which borders on adoration. Idolatry is not just worshipping a god or image other than God, it is lusting after our own desires and pleasures, instead of doing what he wants us to do for him.

The message of rebellion and idolatry are divine warning signals for us to heed so that we may be protected from slipping away from God. Gabriel referred me to I Cor. 10, and let me look at Moses and the children of Israel, who were God's chosen people, to see what took them out from under the cloud covering which is an illustration of the blood covering God places over us today. Verse 1 says, "Moreover, brethren, I would not that ye should be ignorant, how that all our fathers were under the cloud, and all passed through the sea."

They had everything going for them! They were separated from Egypt, which was a type of the world; they were protected and spared; and they had this beautiful covering, the cloud!

Then he said, "And they were all baptized unto Moses in the cloud and in the sea; And did all eat the same spiritual meat; And did all drink the same spiritual drink: for they drank of that spiritual Rock that followed them: and that Rock was Christ. But with many of them God was not well pleased: for they were overthrown in the wilderness." Notice that even though they had supernatural experiences, and the cloud covered them, God was not pleased. Why wasn't he pleased? "For they were overthrown in the wilderness." Why? Because they lusted after evil things! They rebelled against what God had for them and they worshipped the idol of self-pleasure!

What is an evil thing? It's hungering after those things which God says to leave alone because he knows they will bring ultimate destruction.

Look at it from God's written Word: "Now these things were our examples, to the intent we should not lust after evil things, as they also lusted. Neither be ye idolaters, as were some of them; as it is written, The people sat down to eat and drink, and rose up to play. Neither let us commit fornication, as some of them committed, and fell in one day three and twenty thousand" (I Cor. 10:6-8).

They fell into idolatry and put something else in place of

God. They called him Lord but flagrantly failed to do the things he told them to do. The same thing is happening today because there is a false teaching going around the world which says that fornication is not wrong! These false teachers that the Bible warns about are saying that this is an old-fashioned idea of another generation to keep this one from having fun!

This commandment didn't start a generation or two ago; God gave it to the Israelites over 3,000 years ago. He put this in his plan and his Word because he hates this sin, and lets us know that when we rebel against him, we are starting down that road which leads out from under the covering.

A young man and woman who had been "live-in" partners under the new morality recently gave their lives to the Lord. They were excited when they discovered their sins were forgiven, and thought for a while they could continue living in sin. Like many young people today, they had been ensnared by a style of living which condones fornication or other forms of rebellion and idolatry. Praise God, they saw the light and were married shortly afterward!

Some people show an utter lack of respect for what God has said. "Neither let us tempt Christ, as some of them also tempted, and were destroyed of serpents" (I Cor 10:9). God showed his hatred for what they did in disobeying his wishes for them, and when they murmured, God sent his angel to destroy 23,000 of them!

WARNING! "So be careful. If you are thinking, 'Oh, I would never behave like that' — let this be a warning to you. For you too may fall into sin. But remember this — the wrong desires that come into your life aren't anything new and different. Many others have faced exactly the same problems before you. And no temptation is irresistible. You can trust God to keep the temptation from becoming so strong that you can't stand up against it, for he has promised this and will do what he says. He will show you how to escape temptation's power so that you can bear up patiently against it. So, dear friends, carefully avoid idol-worship of every kind" (I Cor. 10:12-24).

Do you see how God's covering works? He does not condone sin, but he wants people to hear the Good News so they can reach out and find the power to be lifted out of these sins. Only those who defy him and walk in their own way find themselves on thin ice because they have paid no attention to his warning signs. God is not looking for reasons to condemn you, and that's the reason he has posted warning signs. His heart cry is, "I want to save you; I want you to have life and have it more abundantly!"

WARNING! There are some definite warning signals in the Word where God highlights his plan, his acceptance and his covering for his people. He is not deleting the warnings and the call to his people to walk with him and to live for him. The warnings that he has given are just as sure as ever, but he wants them to be put in their proper perspective. He wants people who love him and desire to live for him to know how safe they are. But he wants people to know that the path they are on could lead to real trouble if they are not taking him seriously.

Law-abiding people are not worried every day because there happens to be a jail downtown! In fact, they can even walk right up to a policeman, look him in the eye, shake hands and give him a friendly greeting. They don't need to be worried, because they have been obeying the law. That is exactly the way God wants you to feel about him!

WARNING: Beware of a loss of a sense of the importance of spiritual things!

There are many, many believers on the road of lethargy. Lethargy is a sense of lack of importance; a drowsy dullness to God; a lack of spiritual energy; sluggish in activity. Lethargy speaks forth from our inner being when we say, "It's easier to stay home. It's hard to generate excitement and zeal for the things of God. I have a few other things I want to do today, so I just won't go to church!"

God's remedy: "Let us not neglect our church meetings, as some people do, but encourage and warn each other, especially now that the day of his coming back again is drawing near" (Heb. 10:25 TLB). Remember, if you feel numb and cold inside and it's a weight and a burden for you to think, "Here's another weekend and I have to go to church. What a chore!" WATCH OUT! DANGER! THIN ICE!

WARNING! UNBELIEF!

God wants us to have an alive awareness of what he is doing. He wants us to believe in the supernatural, because he is the God of the supernatural. If in your heart you are standing aloof, beware! "(Therefore beware,) brethren; take care lest there be in any one of you a wicked, unbelieving heart — which refuses to cleave to, trust in and rely on Him — leading you to turn away and desert or stand aloof from the living God" (Heb. 3:12 Amp).

You might have had a real interest in church and working for God, but there has crept into your thinking a spirit of skepticism. You stand aloof with unbelief or doubt, both of which are enemies of God. If you say you believe in the supernatural and give one reason why you do and nine why you don't, your words are just hollow echoes. The warning says that you don't really believe in the supernatural, and without even realizing it, you find yourself questioning God's ways in your mind.

It is so easy to be lulled into becoming an observer who stands aloof saying, "I can't get too involved; I'm more or less neutral." There is no neutral ground — you are either pulling one way or another.

We need to be like Peter and Paul and some of the other disciples who followed Jesus and were willing to lay down their lives for God! I'm excited to say that there has never been a time in the history of the world when God's people were more dedicated to what he is doing that they are today.

WARNING: "The backslider in heart shall be filled with his own ways:" (Pro. 14:14).

When you begin drifting back, long before you get totally away from God, you are interested only in those things that pertain to you, not the things of God. This is a warning sign.

WARNING! "What shall we say then? Shall we continue in sin, that grace may abound?" (Rom. 6:1).

The grace of God is a beautiful covering, but it is not a license to sin. God's grace is something we did not earn, something we cannot buy. A person who thinks they can do what they please is rebelling against God and skating on thin ice!

WARNING! ". . . Receive not the grace of God in vain" (II Cor. 6:1).

God's grace is a gift and should not be received in vain. Paul tells about this in connection with what God did in providing his covering, and he gave us this warning: "For God took the sinless Christ and poured into him our sins. Then, in exchange, he poured God's goodness into us! As God's partners we beg you not to toss aside this marvelous message of God's great kindness." God did this for you and what a beautiful word of assurance he is giving, but he warned us not to toss it aside for worldly pleasures. "For God says, 'Your cry came to me at a favorable time, when the doors of welcome were wide open. I helped you on a day when salvation was being offered.' Right now God is ready to welcome you. Today he is ready to save you."

Then he goes on to tell us how we can keep from tossing it aside: "We try to live in such a way that no one will ever be offended or kept back from finding the Lord by the way we act, so that no one can find fault with us and blame it on the Lord. In fact, in everything we do we try to show that we are true ministers of God" (II Cor. 5:21 and 6:1-4 TLB). Hallelujah!

Suppose you just purchased a new dishwasher for your home. You are excited about all the new features and the many hours it will save you in your kitchen, and you are reading the instructions on how to make it do the best job for you. You discover a little sign that says, "WARNING! For the best and most efficient operation, do thus and so."

What would happen if you suddenly thought, "I can't keep this in my home; it may fail me!" Just for a moment you took your eyes off of the benefits and enlarged on the word of caution and immediately all the benefits diminished in your mind!

What God has promised is the same thing for the individual who recognizes what has been done for him and what God wants to do. God's promises and his benefits are all spelled out for him and the equipment is superior. We are sold on how good God is and how his interest in us is told in all of his good promises, not one word of which has he ever failed to perform. His guarantee is unlimited! But there is still a warning sign, and it is there to make it work for you!

A red light flashes at a railroad crossing when the train is coming, to prevent us from getting killed!

A fire engine sounds a siren to warn us of its approach!

An ambulance and a police car flash lights when there is danger, and the wail of their siren warns us to pull over and get out of the way.

A fever warns us of sickness and infection.

All of these signals are good, and so are God's warning signs. They are just as effective to keep us from getting killed (spiritually) as the flashing lights at a railroad crossing are to keep us from getting killed physically! God loves us so much he has posted warning signs all along the lake of joy, just for our protection!

WHEN GOD SAYS THANKS

His eyes were like deep, glowing embers, his voice resonant and clear . . . this giant angel . . . as he told me about "The Believer's Judgment."

My heart leaped when I heard him say, "THE BELIEVER'S JUDGMENT IS NOT A DARK NIGHT THROUGH WHICH HE MUST PASS BEFORE HE BREAKS OUT INTO GOD'S ETERNAL DAY, BUT A DAY IN WHICH GOD HAS CHOSEN TO SAY THANKS TO HIS PEOPLE."

CHAPTER 10

WHEN GOD SAYS THANKS!

There is tremendous joy in my heart, knowing that God cares enough for his people to give them divine guidance and direction. I also feel a profound responsibility to bring to the world the truths which God has placed upon my heart. These are biblical facts which many of us know, but to have God articulate them so clearly and call our attention to them by angelic messengers and other supernatural means, adds an extra weight!

These experiences the Lord has allowed me to have a part in and to share, have not been just empty dreams or imaginations. Every time God has dealt with me, he has brought the Word of God to me with great force and supporting power.

On his first visit to me, this angel spoke of three main areas. The first was God's character, what he is really like, the desires of his heart toward people, and the things that are important to God. The second was our position in God, and third, he wanted me to remind you of the preparation for that great judgment day!

The first area is summarized in the chapter on GOOD NEWS FOR YOU AND YOUR FAMILY!

The second area is the position from which God sees us, and this is covered in the chapter on the ATONEMENT. I asked him, "Where in the Bible can I actually see this at work?" and God said, "I have had it recorded. You can read it in Numbers" (Num. 23:21), and he told me exactly what it meant. He let me know that the sacrifice that Israel had put their trust in, was a type of the great sacrifice of

Christ in which we put our faith, and that it made them accepted by God between the yearly sacrifices.

I had read through the Bible many times and had never seen this beautiful truth of God, stating that he looks at man from a different level than man himself does. God's eyeview is on the top side of this covering; man's eyeview is on the underside.

This has been referred to practically every time God has dealt with me. God wants us to know our position in him. As we desire to live for him, and we WANT him as our Lord, the blood covering is there! He sees us through the covering as the flowers and trees which he has planted himself. He sees us like Christ because we are accepted in him, all wrapped up and covered in his love. With our faith in him, he wants us to know this position. He wants us to know that the day is coming which the Apostle Paul spoke of in II Tim. 1:12 where he said, "I know whom I have believed, and am persuaded that he is able to keep that which I have committed unto him against that day." This will be a day of beauty and a day of reward!

God wants us to be aware of what is important to him. When we know how much he cares about certain things, then we will want to care about them. He says, "Is not this the fast that I have chosen? to loose the bands of wickedness, to undo the heavy burdens, and to let the oppressed go free, and that ye break every yoke?" (Isaiah 58:6-7).

God wants us to be interested in the things he is interested in, and that is people! "Is it not to deal thy bread to the hungry, and that thou bring the poor that are cast out to thy house? when thou seest the naked, that thou cover him; and that thou hide not thyself from thine own flesh?" God is giving us an inside picture of his heart. He is telling us about the things that are REALLY important!

He said people are doing a lot of things that are "good" things, necessary things, things of this life, and things that need to be done. They have a real value while in this life, so they are not worthless. They have a reason here, but they are not all things which are going to remain. He mentioned specifically certain books which people spend all their time writing, books which may have value, but do not meet the needs of people.

Singing performances, unless directed to the need of a life, are temporary and will not go on. Even sermons that are preached which can be giving out information, may be preached to a CROWD of people, but not to the NEED of the people! These may help to guide and motivate people and steer them in a certain direction, but they will not be something that actually remains.

Buildings have a great purpose, but God doesn't need buildings. He has buildings which put those in this old world to shame.

He spoke about "giving" campaigns. He said if you give for credit, you get your reward here, but not in heaven. Often an individual's missionary vision has been hurt because of a desire for credit or recognition. It is all right if people have to be motivated, but this kind of giving is not going down in God's book. He wants giving from the heart! These are the exact words the angel used: "These things may have satisfying reward in this life, and they are important, but they will not remain."

"What will remain?" I questioned.

He referred to Phil. 4:17-18 where Paul told them to bring a gift out of their want. It wasn't that he desired that they bring a gift to him, but as he said, "*I desire fruit* that may abound to your account." So, when this book is open, it will show that these people did something special, not for reward here, but for the Lord.

In John 15:16, Jesus' prayer was that the fruit of your life should remain. God wants us to have something that is in the book forever, because he loves us so very much!

I'm sure this ministering angel has been with me many times before. While I was in the hospital many years ago, I heard a voice while I was very, very sick. The message that came to me almost every day was: "Strengthen those things that remain." Today he is talking about the same thing. He wants us to strengthen those things that last forever.

People are special to God. If you want to know where God lives on this earth, look where people are and you will find his address because God lives where people are hurting. He wants to help them. He involves himself with the needs of people. It is when we get down on the level of human need and take a person into our hearts and actually meet their need that something is written down in our book in heaven.

Other things may help, but the fruit he wants is your personal love, your personal help, and your personal concern. When you see an individual hurting and your own heart actually hurts with them, this is when you care!

Recently, I asked the children in my church, "What is Jesus like?" Look at their answers:

"Jesus is somebody who loves to help you."

"If you are hungry, he will provide food."

"If you are sick, he wants you well!"

"He loves you!"

This is the way little children understand the message from God.

God's desire is that we be like Jesus and we will always find him moving in the areas of human need.

The angel spoke about personal involvement with our own family — with our own flesh and blood. Not what we DO for them, but what we ARE to them. What they mean to us! Some members of our own family may have been real "stinkers." They may have taken advantage of us. They may have lied to us, and we said, "I'm writing that person off." God doesn't want us to hurt that person; he wants our heart to go out and love them and help them in every way we possibly can. That is God's nature.

This message applies not only to our own family, but to the family of God. In Galatians 6:10, it is written that God desires for us to do good to all men, especially to the household of God. He wants us to represent Jesus and to be like him. This is what is recorded in our heavenly account. We can help that person who is lonely! We can help that person who is hurting! We can help that person who may be filled with frustration! Jesus said, "Inasmuch as ye have done it unto one of the least of these my brethren, ye have done it unto me" (Matt. 25:40). These are the deeds which are written in our book.

The angel said it was more important to be like Jesus in meeting the area of a person's need, than to be witnessing to people about salvation. That really surprised me. We have become so conditioned to the idea that we aren't doing anything for God unless we are able to get out and witness and to skillfully use the Word. But this angel said, "When you are helping people, you become a living word to them which says, 'I care and God cares for you!' " That doesn't mean we exalt ourselves as Jesus; it simply means Jesus is living his life through us. We become a word that is alive to them, not a dead, printed word, but a living word. This is something we can do, and it is more important than witnessing, quoting scripture or teaching. Instead of witnessing, we BECOME a witness of what Jesus is really like.

This is something everyone can do! We don't have to have a special talent to lay up treasure in heaven. Any Christian can make a deposit in the bank of heaven every day, because there are people who need help every day! When we care for them, we are bringing the heart of God to them in their place of need. When we do this for God, something goes into our account!

While we are waiting for the coming of Jesus, let's get out and get our book full, not doing it for that specific reason, but doing it because that is the way God's heart beats for people. When we are close to him, we will feel the same way. Things which are done because of his love and his Spirit in us are placed in our account in the archives of heaven!

In Matthew 25:35-40, Jesus taught that when we feed the hungry, give water to the thirsty, and do a service to people, we are doing this as unto him. This includes a visit to a rest home to cheer up a person who is depressed, or caring for a little child whose mother is so weary she can hardly stand. When we have been tired ourselves, but have said, "I want to share this load with you," and haven't looked for a reward, we are doing this as unto Jesus. These deeds are recorded in the book!

We will be doing what Jesus did when we show kindness to individuals by helping them feel their worth when they have been beaten down and are depressed, when their self-worth and their self-esteem has been crushed.

God cares for people, and the only way people will know that he cares is through you and me. That is why it is so important for us to know what he is like. God said not to glory in wealth, or wisdom, or might, or other things of this world, but to glory in this, that you know God, that he is a God of justice and a God filled with kindness.

People often get their thinking confused. They think the only things you do for God are what you do in a spiritual way. When we minister, it might be hard to relate to a person's spirit, but it's not hard to relate to their physical needs, their bodies and their emotions. Jesus always ministered to both spiritual and physical needs.

For example, one day a man came to my office who was involved in homosexuality, a way of life that I hate. I had a real battle with myself. He didn't want prayer and he wouldn't even admit his need for deliverance from homosexuality, but he was hungry. He hadn't had any food for a while. I had to ask myself, "What would Jesus do?" I knew that Jesus would separate the man from his sin, so I did the same, and in peeling away the vileness, I found the signature of God. This man was hungry!

Jesus said, "If your enemy hungers, give him to eat." I have to confess I had a hard time because I thought about people who deserved food more than he did, so I told him, "I know what your life is. You cannot hide it, but you are hungry, and God cares about that, and I care." Then I provided food for him.

I didn't do it to get something recorded, but I know that act of kindness is in God's book. I wasn't doing it for that reason, but when you feel the working of the Spirit in your heart, he gives you love for people, and that is your motive. For "The fruit of the Spirit is love, joy, peace, longsuffering, gentleness, goodness, faith, meekness, temperance" (Gal. 5:22). All of these are traits of God which reach out to people.

I wish I had known a long time ago how God feels about people and how much he loves them. When Jesus walked on this earth, he was searching for people in need, and he is still looking for them. He has multitudes of emissaries walking around, and is saying to them, "I want you to get out there where the need is." When we have lovingly prepared a meal for someone who has been sick, and have brightened up their day by caring, something is being written down in that book.

Caring for those who are not in the family of God is also important. We care when we help the fatherless and the widows who don't know which way to turn because they can't find direction. God said through this angel, "This is pure religion, and it is undefiled. This is what will last and be recorded in the archives of heaven."

I remember some of those hell, fire and brimstone evangelistic sermons that used to make straight hair curl, trying to scare people into heaven. I heard one man say, "God takes all the sins that he is holding in reserve against you and holds them over your head to keep you going straight!" Then he would thunder on, "You're going to have to face every sin because they are all written down in your book and held in reserve. On the day of judgment, God is going to take a big screen and projector and show all your sins to the world, including your family and friends." Then he said, "The wrongs that you did before you were saved are all forgiven, but everything you do after you are saved is kept in reserve to be held against you." People really squirmed when they heard a message like that, and it seemingly moved some people toward God, but praise God, it isn't true!

As the angel gave me this message, he said that this is in conflict and contrary to the character of God. When you confess your sin, he destroys it, wipes it out, and says he will never, never remember it again. If you have been deceived into believing that on that glorious day of judgment a lot of condemnation is going to be brought against you, I have good news for you! It simply will not happen that way. It's going to be a BEAUTIFUL day when, instead of judgmental condemnation, God says, "THANKS!"

Christ is our foundation. Nothing can move him. Your faith and trust in Jesus puts you on a foundation that can never be destroyed. God tells us that all we have done which is like Jesus will be permanent and lasting.

Luke said (Luke 3:17) that God is going to separate the chaff from the wheat on that day. He is looking for the kernel that is going to last! The angel actually made the statement that "God is not interested in the chaff." He has no use for it; he is removing it from your life so only that which is perfect, that which is like Jesus, will remain. All he is interested in is what is inside of that chaff — he wants that little kernel and is going to remove the shell and find the life inside that will last forever! Hallelujah!

In I Cor. 3:12, the apostle Paul made reference to the foundation that is going to last forever: "Now if any man build upon this foundation gold, silver, precious stones, wood, hay, stubble; Every man's work shall be made manifest: for the day shall declare it, because it shall be revealed by fire; and the fire shall try every man's work of what sort it is." He refers to the removal and burning of the chaff, revealing that which will last forever.

The things of this life are going to pass away on that

great judgment day, but to the believer it will be a time of great reward where God brings praise to his people. There is not going to be a person present at this believers' judgment who will hear one harsh word of condemnation, because Jesus has already paid our penalty through his death.

As the light of heaven begins to glow before us, and the things of this earth begin to melt and fall away, there is going to emerge a body of believers from all different levels of spiritual growth and spiritual life. All of the things which are transitory are going to be gone, and those who have pleased God will stand on that firm foundation in the eyes of God!

This day is special to God. It is a day that he has looked forward to for a long time. This is the day Paul talked about when he said he knew he could trust God to keep those things which he had committed to him against that day! He continues in I Cor. 4:5 where he says, "Therefore judge nothing before the time, until the Lord come, who both will bring to light the hidden things of darkness, and will make manifest the counsels of the hearts: and then shall every man have PRAISE OF GOD!" "At that time God will give to each one whatever praise is coming to him" (TLB).

Every person is going to hear those words, "Thank you, thank you! You did a good job." Some people do more than others, but EVERYBODY there will have praise of God.

"Then shall EVERY man have praise of God." The apostle Paul said that the day was going to declare it. All the beautiful things God has written down for you are going to be known on that glorious day. God doesn't do things that aren't important, so think what it will mean to him when he takes your hand as you stand before him, looks you in the eye, and says "Thanks! Thanks for all those things you did for me!" Every Christian is going to hear those words, "Thank you! You did a good job!"

My human mind could not comprehend how God could ever say thank you to me. I shall never forget the awesomeness of the moment when the angel told me that on that glorious day, God would say those words, because it is beyond my ability to understand that God could love me so much that he would ever say, "Thank you, Roland Buck!"

I asked the angel to explain what is meant by "things of darkness and the counsels of the hearts," and this was his answer: "God will shine his light on the hidden corners of the hearts of those who have served him because of their love, not expecting thanks. For these things, too, they will hear God say thanks." This does not mean in relation to evil deeds. The angel referred to it as the beautiful, but hidden things that people have not known about your life. God is going to tell you good things that you don't even know about yourself! He knows all of your thoughts, and even those good thoughts are worthy of praise!

I don't know when Jesus is coming. How I wish the angel had given me some indication, but he didn't. Events pointing toward his coming are happening fast, however, and angels are moving hindrances out of the way. People are being moved about and touched by God more than I have ever witnessed before.

Many more people are going to be saved and turn to God when they see us doing God's work for him by meeting their needs, than when we are trying to put the "bee" on them for salvation. People are spiritually hungry. They are longing for someone who actually becomes a living word expressed right in front of them. This is something everyone can do, not just a few skilled people, because we can all beam out that love of God.

When you know God is going to say "thanks" to you some day, doesn't it make you feel like finding someone in need and helping them?

God has put great emphasis on family relationships through these messages brought by the angels. Maybe you have some members of your family you haven't talked to for a long time. Why not give them a call and say, "I'm excited! I believe our circle up there is going to be unbroken because God is working to bring whole families to himself." Sometimes the people in our own family seem to be the most difficult ones to talk to, but among the easiest to whom we can show the love of Jesus.

What this world needs is Jesus! Just a glimpse of him, and it is through us that they can see him.

The last thing the angel said on this subject was that the real desires of our heart and the longings that we have in this life will be met when we take care of another's need in the place of Jesus. The angel stated that we could see what God's interests really are in the fifty-eighth chapter of Isaiah. I read it, and sure enough, it was written right there in the Bible just as he had been telling me.

"No, the kind of fast I want is that you stop oppressing those who work for you and treat them fairly and give them what they earn. I want you to share your food with the hungry and bring right into your own homes those who are helpless, poor and destitute. Clothe those who are cold and don't hide from relatives who need your help. If you do these things, God will shed his own glorious light upon you. He will heal you; your godliness will lead you forward, and goodness will be a shield before you, and the glory of the Lord will protect you from behind. Then, when you call, the Lord will answer. 'Yes, I am here,' he will quickly reply. All you need to do is to stop oppressing the weak, and to stop making false accusations and spreading vicious rumors!

"Feed the hungry! Help those in trouble! Then your light will shine out from the darkness, and the darkness around you shall be as bright as day. And the Lord will guide you continually, and satisfy you with all good things, and keep you healthy too; and you will be like a well-watered garden, like an everflowing spring" (Isa. 58:6-11 TLB).

At the same time you are reflecting Jesus by these acts of kindness, let the message of salvation bubble out of you like a well-watered garden, like an everflowing spring. This is what Jesus did. He never forgot the spiritual needs of people, and neither can we! Both are vital!

When we are giving love and concern to people, God is writing in the archives of heaven those acts for which he will say to each of us, "THANKS!"

Isn't it almost more than our finite minds can understand to know that on that great day, God will greet us with a big welcome and say, "Well done, my good and faithful servant. Thanks!"

MISSION PHILIPPINES

... About four in the morning, the light came on in my room, and I opened my eyes ... There were two cots in the room. I was sleeping in one, and when I looked over at the empty one, I saw Gabriel sitting there.

"How did you find me here?"

"We didn't have any trouble finding you, because we arranged for you to be here!" Gabriel replied.

CHAPTER 11

MISSION PHILIPPINES

It's a strange feeling to be sitting in the San Francisco airport on the way to a foreign country, wondering what's going to happen when you get there! That's the way I felt on the Saturday night I was utterly compelled to go to the Philippines.

The week before I was to leave on this mission, the angel Gabriel met me, spoke with me about the work, and gave me assurance in my heart that what was happening was something that God himself had planned. He gave me the names of people to whom he had been ministering, that he said I would meet, some of whom were not necessarily important to the mission, but were given as a confirmation to me that this trip was from God, and that it was not just a visit!

The plane was scheduled to depart at midnight, and I had a six-and-one-half hour layover. About eleven o'clock I checked in to receive my seat assignment, sat down in the predeparture area and watched the people as they milled around. Spiritually I was tuned in all the way to see what God was doing, and I had a tremendous feeling of anticipation!

There was an empty seat beside me, and a young Filipino sat down. We had an interesting conversation and when we boarded the plane, I discovered this same man was sitting next to me! I immediately got out the list of names given me by Gabriel to check things out. The name S-A-R-I-A-N-O was at the very top of the list. I took a deep breath, asked this young man if Sä-ree-on-ō was the correct way to pronounce his name, and I wish you could have seen the look on his face! He was extremely upset because I knew his name! He looked around to see if there was anything on his person that would identify him, but there was nothing! He quickly got up and took a seat in another part of the plane, which was not full. I had his seat and mine, so I slept all the way to Hawaii.

Prior to departure from Hawaii, the stewardess announced that everyone must take their assigned seats because of the new passengers coming aboard. Reluctantly, this young man came back to sit down beside me, so I thought it would be well to calm him down. I certainly didn't want him to be uneasy for the entire ten-hour flight because that's a long time to be miserable.

I simply and honestly told him I knew his name because it had been given to me by the angel Gabriel. When I said this, he looked around again, but there were no empty seats, and there was no place for him to go! I told him that God loved him and that this trip was going to be more than a visit, because he had been chosen to carry some good news to his family. I also told him that God had his eye on him, had known him all along and cared for him.

He said, "How could God know me? I don't know him. I go to the priest and the priest probably tells God about me, but I don't really know God." I explained to him that God knew him, that God had prepared him and had directed this entire trip, and had even given me his name. Then I said that God had also seen to it that when the seats were assigned to the 300 people on the plane, his seat would be right next to mine!

His eyes were wide with astonishment as I told him these things, and he said, "Do you mean that God is really interested in me, with all that he has to do? Do you mean that God really cares about someone who doesn't even know him?" I answered, "Yes, he wants you to commit your life to him, in order to let him know that you are thankful to him for his concern for you, as great as he is, and as insignificant as you are."

Right then and there this young man accepted Jesus as his Savior and Lord! He excitedly said, "Let me tell you about my father and my family. I remember many times as my father would look up into the night sky and see the stars, he would say, 'Surely there must be a God, someplace, if only we could find him.' " Then he continued, "Now I'm going to go back and tell him that he was right, there is a God, and that I have found him."

Then I asked him about his family. I thought when he referred to his family that he was referring to his immediate family. He continued on, "All of my family are going to be together because they live in a little cluster. When I left thirteen years ago to go to the United States, there were about 400 members in my family. I don't know how large it is now, probably 700, or maybe even more than that, but I'm going to tell them all! They are going to know that God loves each and every one of them!"

This really excited me, because then he added, "If the angels are interested in me, don't you suppose they are interested in my family too? Is it all right if I tell them?"

"Sure, that's what God wants you to do. God is so interested in your family that he gave me your name. You are going back there as God's representative."

With great emotion, he looked me straight in the eye, and said, "This is the most serious, the most important task I've ever had." He knew it was special because he recognized the fact that I had no way of getting his name, except from God, and he became an instant missionary!

The Philippine trip was one of the 120 events God had told me would occur, but nothing happened until two months prior to my actual departure date, when I received an invitation to come to the Philippines. I immediately checked the cost of the trip and my estimate was $1,730.00. How was God going to supply the money? It didn't take long to find out, because the very next day a check came for $1,730.00 from an unexpected source!

Gabriel had met me in my office at church to give me the instructions for this mission to the Philippines. At that time he looked very serious as he paced back and forth, almost as if he were troubled. He reflected God's concern over the fact that people would hear the message of going into all the world and then go back to sleep. This trip was definitely not just a spur-of-the-moment thing, but was in the unfolding of God's plan.

He said my message would be from the 96th chapter of Psalms and 97:1,2: "Sing a new song to the Lord! Sing it everywhere around the world! Sing out his praises! Bless his name. Each day tell someone that he saves.

"Publish his glorious acts throughout the earth. Tell everyone about the amazing things he does. For the Lord is great beyond description, and greatly to be praised. Worship only him among the gods! For the gods of other nations are merely idols, but our God made the heavens! Honor and majesty surround him; strength and beauty are in his Temple.

"O nations of the world, confess that God alone is glorious and strong. Give him the glory he deserves! Bring your offering and come to worship him. Worship the Lord with the beauty of holy lives. Let the earth tremble before him. Tell the nations that Jehovah reigns! He rules the world. His power can never be overthrown. He will judge all nations fairly.

"Let the heavens be glad, the earth rejoice; let the vastness of the roaring seas demonstrate his glory. Praise him for the growing fields, for they display his greatness. Let the trees of the forest rustle with praise. For the Lord is coming to judge the earth; he will judge the nations fairly and with truth!

"JEHOVAH IS KING! Let all the earth rejoice! *Tell the farthest islands to be glad.* Clouds and darkness surround him. Righteousness and justice are the foundation of his throne" (TLB).

Sunday was an unusual day. My first service was at the Holiday Inn, and was a part of International Hotel Ministries, a world-wide organization. The auditorium was packed with what looked like top-of-the-line citizens. This was very interesting to me, because I had pictured the Philippines as being a place of poverty, a place where I was going to see the gospel really work in the raw. Yet here was my first introduction to the Philippines, and it was in one of the fanciest, nicest buildings I have ever been in throughout my entire life. Men were dressed in beautiful suits and ties, and the women were exquisitely gowned. They had their black hair wound up high on their head, and were such sophisticated looking people, I wondered if I had actually just made a few circles around one of the big American cities and landed! They looked like they were from anywhere except the Philippine Islands!

My second service was on Sunday night at the Faith Assembly in Manila. When I walked into this church, I didn't see any of the wealth I had seen in the morning service, but I did see people here who really loved God, in spite of their poverty. This building was in an area of tremendous crime and violence. Every window had bars just like a jail. What a difference in surroundings from the morning service!

I was staying at the guest house of the Wycliff Translators. It's a big place, a compound, and they have about 70 guests at a time. God had allowed me to stay there to fellowship and minister to these people who have dedicated their lives to learning the languages of tribes who have no written language, giving them a written language, and then translating the Bible into those languages. God had arranged for me to meet with perhaps the most significant group in the country in reaching the far-flung tribes. There were doctors, pilots, college professors, teachers and other leaders pooling their efforts to reach the island population.

Later I spoke about angelic visitations to a group of missionaries during an evening service. As I was speaking, I realized that it might be something so new to them that it could be a little difficult to accept. God also knew this, and he knew exactly what to do about the situation! During the prayer time, the president of the Bible school felt a heavy hand on his shoulder, and he thought possibly someone had put their hand on him to pray for him. He looked around to see who it was, but there was no one there! He said to the people, "This is real, it's real! God has confirmed it. Even though I can't see him, I KNOW this angel's hand is upon my shoulder." He and his wife stayed up most of the night talking about how he had felt the divine hand of God as this angel reached out and gripped his arm. I hadn't seen Gabriel there, but it was interesting to know that he was around and had found his way to the Philippine Islands!

It was there I received my schedule of meetings for this trip. I was troubled when I looked at it, because I saw that seven whole days were going to be spent in only two churches. I hadn't fully analyzed ahead of time what I was going to be doing, but this information really surprised me! I wondered why I had come all the way over here just to do that! If all I was going to do was speak in two churches, I could have done that back in Idaho!

I had been talking to the people at the Wycliff guest house and they were telling me exciting stories of being among the tribes who didn't know any English at all. They were completely uncivilized and many of them just wore G-strings. They still carried bows and arrows, and their darts had poison in them. I was very interested in this, feeling it might be the reason for my trip, and it did prove to be an important part, but not in the way I expected it to be!

On Monday I met with one medical doctor, a college professor, and two pilots. They had just returned from Mindanao where there is a tribe which had been discovered just a year-and-a-half previously. They were way back in the jungles, and while this group had been there, the professor was able to put together some type of a communication bridge to them. I explained to them that God had sent me to the Philippines, and they said, "We had come here for a little rest, but we don't need the rest, let's go back tomorrow! We want to take YOU down there! God's in this!"

I really got excited until I realized that it was impossible for me to go because I was scheduled elsewhere. I kept trying to think of ways to clear my schedule so I could go. They had a plane which would fly me to the airfield closest to this particular tribe. At that airfield they had a helicopter pilot who could fly me inland. They kept saying, "We want you to go!" But I couldn't, because it wasn't on the itinerary to which I was committed!

I went to bed Monday night thinking, "I've really muffed it! I got ahead of God in telling them to arrange a schedule for me. God really wanted me to come over here and help this brand new tribe, and I missed it! I can't get out of this now, because the meetings have already been advertised!"

It was hot and sticky in the place, very difficult to sleep, and my mind kept whipping me so badly I couldn't sleep anyway! I pulled the sheet up into a big, old knot as I wrestled and wrestled with this problem until about two o'clock in the morning, when I finally went to sleep.

About four in the morning, the light came on in my room, and I opened my eyes. The guest house was very plainly furnished and there were just two cots in a room. I was sleeping in one, and when I looked over at the empty one, I saw Gabriel sitting there with Chrioni, the angel who travels with him. I was so sleepy, I said, "How did you find me here?" Normally I wouldn't have talked to them the way I did, but I was so groggy from sleep I forgot that when God has sent someone on assignment to represent him, you don't question them.

Gabriel said, "We didn't have any trouble finding you, because we arranged for you to be here! We had a reason.

We want you to mingle with these people so they can get a good grip on this message and take it back to their area." This made me feel better, and then he said, "The reason we have come is that God has sensed the concern in your heart that you might be wasting your time over here with these churches, and he wants us to tell you not to be concerned about that schedule, because it is so ordered and arranged that every person who meets with you will be divinely selected. They have been personally selected by God to hear what you have to say."

It was interesting to me to realize that regardless of whether I was in one spot or another, whoever was going to be there was there at God's direction, so I didn't concern myself about it any more. I wondered who God was going to bring, so I began looking and anticipating. I was tempted to do a few things myself just to try to work things out, but I didn't. I decided that I might be out doing something when I should be waiting and watching what God was doing!

While in Manila, I spoke at the Far East Advanced School of Theology, and I realized that this also was in God's order. The young people attending this Bible college are from Southeast Asia, and the impact from this school covers that entire part of the world. God had arranged things so that his messages would work up from the roots of the Philippine Islands through the Wycliff workers, and now he had arranged for it to go to different places in Asia. Students were there from Burma which is now closed to western missionaries.

I went down to Iloilo where my sponsors put me in the best hotel available. It was several miles to the business section, or the market place as they call it, and I wondered what was going to happen here. I thought, "Well, if what the angels told me is true (and who would doubt angels?), they will bring people around. I don't know who they will bring, but at least I know that they know where I am."

I didn't stay in my room very much. I went down to the lobby and sat there watching everything and everybody, because I wanted to be in the right place at the right time. Nothing much happened the first evening.

The next morning I went down to breakfast, and God's beautiful plan began to unfold. Two businessmen were sitting at a table, and they said, "We saw you here last night and wondered what you were doing here. You don't look like a tourist to us, so why don't you sit with us and tell us why you are here."

I sat down and started the conversation by saying, "Gentlemen, I don't know what your background is, so I don't know whether or not you are going to accept this, but an angel told me that everyone that I speak with has been especially selected by God to hear what I have to say, so I believe that you two men have been selected by God."

They looked at me as though they didn't quite believe what I was saying, so then I said, "The fact that you have been selected is because your training or your background, whatever it is, has been directed by God, and God is calling it into account at this time. He doesn't do things promiscuously, and he has selected you for something special. I don't know what it is, but I do know that he has selected you. This is his plan and his purpose. He wants what you have and what he has given you, because everything you have has been given to you by God, whether you know him or not."

These men looked at each other, and one of them said, "It sounds strange, but we believe you, so if we have been selected, what is the next step?"

I knew what the next step would be, but I thought that possibly I would have to argue with them a little bit, but here they were, ready to go on. I said, "God wants you to say, 'All right, God, here I am. I am glad that you care enough for me that you want to do something with my life. I'm ready to do what you want me to, and here is my life. I accept you.'"

These men, with no question mark in their minds whatsoever, felt that what I was telling them was directly from God, and without any hesitation at all, both of them raised their hands and said, "God, we want to put our hands in yours. If we have something that you have given to us that you can use, we give it to you. We want you to use us!"

I talked to them for a few minutes, then together we talked to God. We worshipped and praised him for the supernatural way he works. Then they said, "We are here on special business, and all of our training has been in the area of politics and government control, and we are giving the rest of our lives to God in order to help people."

I mentioned to them that the angel had told me that my ministry would be in the area of liberation. I said, "God is smiling on the Philippine Islands, and he is bringing liberation to spirit, soul and body. He is raising up pastors who are going to help free people's spirits." Then I added, "They are impoverished; they are oppressed; these people have been under oppressors for hundreds of years. First were the Chinese, the Spanish, the Americans, then the Japanese, then the Americans again, and now the Filipino government. They have been under the heel of an oppressor and God wants to set them free!"

The men said, "We are in that position. We are going to put some wheels in motion to set them free." I couldn't help but say, "Hallelujah!" I hadn't planned on saying it, but all I knew was that God was concerned about the needs of the whole being of these people and that he was smiling on them.

On Monday morning, I met a man in the hotel lobby. He kept staring at me, so I thought I would go over to see if he had been selected by God. He looked like an American, so I walked over and said, "You look like an American to me." He told me he was German. I told him that a good number of Americans are of German descent. Then he asked me, "What are you doing here?" Hallelujah! God had given me the same opportunity I previously had with the two businessmen.

I started off the same way, "I don't know whether you will believe this or not, but an angel met me and told me that those people with whom I would talk in the Philippines had been selected by God for a special assignment. I don't know how you are going to take this, but you have been selected to hear what I have to say."

Then I continued and told him the same thing, that God had use for all of his training and background. This man opened his heart and said, "I never realized that God really cared that much about what I did, but I would like to have more purpose in my life."

I told him that the Lord had use for his talents, his training and his skills and that he wanted him to turn his life over to him. Without any question at all, he immediately accepted the Lord! Then I noticed that he was sobbing and softly speaking to God. His eyes were open and he was looking up with both hands in the air and said, "God, just think, I've only been in the Philippine Islands one day and already I have a new boss!"

I asked him what brought him to the Philippines. He had been sent to the islands by the World Committee of the United Nations to develop food resources for the impoverished and underfed people of the land. I told him that the people selected by God were involved in the liberation of these poor people. Then I said to him, "You, in your position now, are going to help liberate bondages of hunger." He said, "That's the thing I have been skilled at and trained for, so I give myself to the Lord for this!"

From Iloilo I went to the island of Negros by ship. My hotel was in the middle of the city, and I didn't tell anyone, including the pastor, what I was doing in the daytime. I looked at the people, and my heart went out to them, but I couldn't communicate with them because even though quite a number of the people speak broken English, I nudged a lot of people and couldn't find anyone who really spoke English. Finally, I found one young man who could speak quite well, or at least he could get by. He was just twenty-one years old, and he stayed with me the entire time I was there. If I came out of the hotel at 5:30 in the morning, he was standing on the steps waiting for me. God divinely put him there as an interpreter to allow me to communicate with the people, because the ones I really wanted to reach could not understand me at all!

The first day as we walked down the street I noticed a well-dressed lady weeping, with a towel held over her face. I discovered she was the owner of one of the stores there. I could see her shoulders heave as she sobbed.

I said, "Why are you crying, lady?"

She didn't answer, but kept sobbing, so I said, "I'm here to help you. I'm a pastor, and I want to help you. God loves you and he cares about your need." I waited as the interpreter relayed what I had said.

"Tell the man it is not important."

The boy interpreted, and I said, "Anything that is important to you is important to God," so she took the towel off her face. She had been crying a long time and her eyes were red. I took her hands and prayed that God would put his strong arms around her and help her with whatever her need was. As she lifted her head, it looked as though the clouds were pushed back, and the sun had come up!

"Ask him if his name is Jesus! I've cried many times before, but nobody has ever cared, and this man did!"

I was violating the rules that you get as a tourist or a missionary, because they give you a lot of do's and don't's, and you are not supposed to interfere in anyone's business. I wasn't aware of it, but the people in the crowded market places were beginning to gather around to see what was going on. Before long, it was noised around the whole market place that I cared for this woman!

The next violation occurred when I saw a lady carrying a heavy bag of rice which looked like it weighed about eighty pounds. She was extremely old and her legs were badly bowed, so I asked her how far she had to carry the bag. She replied that it was about two miles. I probably could have asked the young man to carry the bag for the lady, but I took the bag of rice myself and carried it for her. People saw this, and whispering started in that city of about 360,000 people.

As I went back through the market place, people started following me. They stopped and asked me to please talk to them. On different occasions, as I was simply sharing God's love and concern with people, I noticed they were healed of many afflictions, including some who were badly twisted with arthritis. I wasn't talking about healing to them, I wasn't praying for them, I was just telling them about Jesus and how much he cared for them. There were some deaf mutes who were healed without prayer of any kind. They couldn't hear what I was saying, because they were deaf, and they couldn't have told anyone about it because they were mute, but the Lord healed them and they could both speak and hear!

God proved that those people were selected by him, because after that they really made a run on my hotel, and it certainly became a busy place. They came day after day while I was there and I prayed for them in the lobby of the hotel and ministered to them.

Then came the news that a killer typhoon was scheduled to hit Bocolod at about 8 PM. Already the rain was pelting down fiercely. I told the people to stay at the church because the construction there was much stronger than their flimsy houses which I felt would blow over. For a couple of hours I thought that the typhoon had actually hit. It sounded like jet planes were going overhead, but this was caused by the winds which preceded the full force of the typhoon.

I told the people to stop worrying because it would be no problem for the Lord to bend that typhoon and make it turn around. After all, God is still God! These people have

always lived with fear because there are about twenty
typhoons a year which hit the Philippine Islands, and this
was the worst they had had for many years. It was called a
"killer" typhoon, and they were frightened!

About 7:30 we gathered around the front of the church,
worshipping God and praying. We asked the Lord to bend
that typhoon in a different direction because it was just a
short distance away at that time. Praise God, the Lord
intervened and it swerved over a spot which wasn't inhab-
ited. Hallelujah!

The center of the typhoon which would have knocked
down the buildings and houses completely missed that area.
It also missed Manila, and went over a spot where it wasn't
heavily populated, just as if there had been divine inter-
vention! If it had struck the heavily populated city of
Manila, there would have been literally hundreds of thousands of deaths. The rain and the wind made over 270,000
families homeless, but the killer part missed and went over
the rice fields. The rice was knocked out, but the people
were alive! It's a beautiful thing to watch the Lord in
action!

On my last night I was getting ready to return home via
Manila when I got the word, "Flight canceled." I thought,
"How long will Typhoon Rita last? What about my reservations from here to Manila? Are they now obsolete? What
about my reservation out of Manila?"

It didn't take long to find out. My reservations were now
obsolete and all flights were full until Wednesday. My
reservation out of Manila was also forfeited. I wondered
how long it would take me to get another. Then I thought,
"Why worry? God knows! He is the one who brought me
here."

At one o'clock I called the airport at Manila. The streets
were full of water and the winds were reaching gusts up to
196 miles per hour. There was no chance for reservations.
Seven to ten days at the earliest. I thought of one of the
men God had put in my path who had given me his card.

He had said if I ever needed help to use his card and his name. I needed help now, so I decided to see what would happen. When I gave his name and his conversation, wheels began to turn. Within minutes a seat had been provided, and connections were made for top priority clearance. God knew I would need this help!

I arrived in Manila about noon. Trees and houses were down. The flooding was so bad that from the air it looked like the city was in the sea. Literally tens of thousands of people were seeking passage. I was the only one without previous reservations to be booked to the United States. Thanks to God who sent the government official, I was billed as an unlisted, special passenger.

Special note: ALL the names which Gabriel had given me were identified while I was in the Philippines!

MICHAEL AND HIS ANGELS

I heard loud noises downstairs very early one Monday morning . . .

I will never forget the sight in my living room as I went to investigate . . . Angelic warfare was being directed from my home as the Command post . . . Orders were being received, commands given . . . this attack was serious enough for Michael, the leader of all warring angels, to appear on the scene.

CHAPTER 12

MICHAEL AND HIS ANGELS

About two o'clock one Monday morning, I was awakened when I heard noises in the downstairs part of my house. I immediately investigated to find the cause. When I did, I saw one of the most awesome sights I've ever seen. Standing in my living room were four great warrior angels, and there was tremendous activity going on in my house. Every time God has revealed himself through the visits of angels to my home or study, it has been awesome, but this seemed to be still more staggering because there was a real awareness in my spirit of the importance of what God was doing.

Gabriel met me at the foot of the stairs and asked me to come into the family room. He said, "I don't want you to be frightened or fearful, but Satanic forces have started an attack against you. Just as God has his angelic organization, Satan also has his organization with princes of darkness, although he doesn't have as many, and they are not as powerful. They are not omnipresent and they cannot be everywhere at once. Their doom is already spelled out."

I listened intently to Gabriel as he said he wanted to give me this assurance so that I could strengthen the bonds of God's people, and remind them of the very special time in which we are living. He said that Satan is aware of the fact that God is doing something in Boise, and he has sent princes of darkness to this area in an endeavor to hurt and rob people, to fill their minds with the things of the world and to try to hinder the work of God.

He reminded me of the time when Israel was going to be delivered out of the land of Egypt, that the princes of darkness tried to stop and hinder God's work by killing all the baby boys, hoping to kill Moses. He did the same thing after Jesus was born.

I thought it was extremely interesting when Gabriel said that Satan does not know what is going to happen. He cannot foretell the future and he cannot read the minds of people. He is extremely nervous because he doesn't know exactly what is going on, but he is hoping somehow to slow down whatever it is that God is doing! Gabriel said since the Holy Spirit monitors everything on earth, he will not allow him to do this. When he sees the activity of Satan becoming dangerous, he dispatches hosts of angels to straighten out the situation.

My attention was drawn to a special angel there, who was very huge and warlike! As I looked at him, I noticed that in spite of this fierceness, there was also a tremendous resemblance to Gabriel! I will never forget the eyes of this large angel because they looked like pools of fire! I was observing his strength and might when Gabriel very simply told me that God had sent his mightiest warring angel to clear away and push back those princes of darkness. I could hardly breathe, it was so awe-inspiring, because this was my introduction to MICHAEL!

It is virtually impossible to describe the radiation and the glow that came from their presence. I could sense compassion and love, and the fruit of the Holy Spirit, because the atmosphere of heaven is the nature of Jesus. All of these angelic beings have that same nature and tremendous compassion.

Gabriel told me that God had given Michael some words for me. I listened with awe! It was real! There was no way I could question it. I was there!

Gabriel informed me that a battle was going on that night and these warring angels in the living room were actually directing the armies of heaven who were pushing back the forces of darkness. Michael and the three captains who were there with him were receiving messages from the Holy Spirit, as he monitored all of the activities, and in turn they were giving messages in languages I didn't understand, to angel leaders who were carrying out the battle.

Michael said that until the appointed time when Satan would be cast out completely, God allows this, and there is a constant dispersing and scattering of evil forces by the warring angels. He told me there was nothing to fear because the angels were overcoming the enemy, guarding and protecting us! Hallelujah!

Michael talked with me quite at length about something I had previously never put in its proper perspective. When God brings truth, we have to forget our little boxes of doctrine, for God can DO what he wants, and KNOWS what he wants to do.

Michael said, "Up until the appointed time, our task is not to destroy Satan, but to scatter the forces of darkness, to hold them in abeyance, to overcome them and to keep them from God's people."

Then he said, "I have an assignment that I am anxiously awaiting where I am not going to have to show respect for Lucifer any more. That assignment is to sweep the heavens clean of Satan and every single one of his angels. We will not leave even one!"

He said, "In case you are not aware of it, twenty-four hours a day there is some type of evil force accusing God's people of things he has already forgiven." Satan does not see things the way God sees them. He knows they are forgiven, but he keeps on accusing them anyway. "But," he said, "The heavens will be swept clean! Lucifer is going to try to fight, but he doesn't have a chance. If you want to read about what is coming, it is found in the twelfth chapter of Revelation, verses seven through ten."

This was the first time I realized that Michael had angels he commanded. The Word says, "Then there was war in heaven; Michael and the angels under his command fought against the Dragon and his host of fallen angels. And the Dragon lost the battle and was forced from heaven.

"This great Dragon — the ancient serpent called the devil, or Satan, the one deceiving the whole world — was thrown down onto the earth with all his army.

"Then I heard a loud voice shouting across the heavens, 'It has happened at last! God's salvation and the power and the rule, and the authority of his Christ are finally here; for the Accuser of our brothers has been thrown down from heaven onto earth — he accused them day and night before our God. They defeated him by the blood of the Lamb, and by their testimony; for they did not love their lives but laid them down for him. Rejoice, O heavens! You citizens of heaven, rejoice! Be glad! But woe to you people of the world, for the devil has come down to you in great anger, knowing that he has little time" (Rev. 12:9-12 TLB).

Satan and his troops cannot do anything to spoil God's plan. During the tribulation, the days will be horrible because all of the fallen angels will be on the earth. Praise God he is taking us out before this happens.

Michael said, "There will not be a place in all of the vast heavens for even one of those demons, not even one!" He emphasized this and said that it is his assignment, and he is ready to go on it as soon as the day is appointed!

Gabriel told me to share this news to encourage the hearts of God's people. He has his eye on them! He has his eye on the whole world; he hasn't given it up to Satan, and he wants us to look at things through his eyes. We might think things look dark, but God wants us to know that he is in control.

Gabriel and Michael both told me that the previous Sunday the princes of darkness were so close that the warring angels stationed themselves in our church service to make sure the enemy couldn't get in. Hallelujah! I rejoiced when he said he would leave his angels as long as they were needed.

Michael had come directly from the presence of God, and the power and force in my house was so strong that most of the day had gone by before I regained my strength. The human body is not made to contain the force that radiates from an angel like Michael, and it certainly had an impact on me!

It is hard for the human mind to comprehend what is actually taking place, and it sounds strange, but the creator of the heavens and the earth is doing something special. These mighty angels cannot come, they cannot appear, and they cannot speak until God says, "Go!" And he is saying it today!

I sensed more of a fierce countenance in Michael than in Gabriel, even though there was a definite resemblance. He had fine, chiseled features, and the description which Daniel gave of the angelic beings was even more complete when I noticed Michael was dressed somewhat like Gabriel. His white tunic had a type of elegant gold embroidery on it, and he wore a wide, gold belt. He wore a type of sandal, and his feet were the color of someone with a deep tan. Daniel said, "It was like burnished brass." His hands and arms also shone. The copper color of his skin was unusual because it was brilliant with the radiation that flows out of him from having been in the presence of God. There was such a definite command about him that I could see what it would mean to any force coming against him!

His hair is light, almost flaxen. He appears to be about twenty-five years old, so it's hard to realize that he is older than the earth!

The other warring angels wore a type of brown tunic, or shirt, tied at the neck with what appeared to be a shoelace. This was worn over very loose trousers.

Angels of God have different ranks. Gabriel is the leading angel, and he stands in the presence of God as a coordinator. God's organization is highly structured and is absolutely beautiful!

Ministering spirits are angels who live right here on this earth with us. God says they encamp around us. They are helping all the time by ministering to us and removing hurts and cares. They know the objections, the strains and the pressures of life, and they are around to help us. They carry the very heartbeat of God, his love, his care and his concern. They live in angelic communities and may appear as ordinary humans. They do not have the strong radiation of the heavenly angels. Seraphims and cherubims are two other kinds of angels.

Right now there is a special task force of angels on special assignments who will not listen to objections of any kind. Gabriel leads them, and they are really busy bringing the lost to believers who will share God's message of salvation with them.

Michael is head of all the great warring angels who do battle with the forces of darkness. Chrioni is a captain of the Lord's hosts and is one of the leading warrior angels.

Many angels have a rank or position in the heavenly army similar to a general or captain. Each one has his own responsibilities with a chain of command under him. When Lucifer fell, he took a section of angels of different ranks with him, so he also has a chain of command, which means there are also various levels of demons.

The Word speaks of the princes of darkness. They are the highest in Satan's army. At any time in history, when Satan knew that God was doing something special, he gathered the princes of darkness together and used all the strategy possible in a special delaying tactic to hurt God's work.

For example, when Daniel was being contacted, the princes of darkness wanted, if possible, to stop the message God was sending to him. Gabriel came against this great force for twenty-one days, and was delayed because the demons had gathered to hinder him in coming. Finally the Holy Spirit sent Michael, the great angel who is in command of all the warring angels.

Because of Michael's tremendous spiritual might, he was able to push back all of those forces of darkness. Then Gabriel got through. When he was talking to Daniel, he said, "Daniel, I couldn't get through for twenty-one days, but then Michael came, and all it took was Michael to stand with me to push them back!"

God is doing something very special now! He has chosen a place to pour out his message, his word and his special insight for this day, just as he did in Daniel's time. There is no question about it, Boise, Idaho, is a touchdown place for angelic beings. Satan has recognized that. He doesn't know what it is all about, but he has brought princes of darkness to this area to try to stop it. But he can't win!

Later that night when they were ready to leave the house, Michael and another of the angels opened our sliding patio doors leading to the back yard. It had snowed about six inches while they were here. They took three steps, which pressed the snow down all the way to the ground, and carried them close to fifteen feet, nearly five feet per step, and then suddenly they disappeared — completely vanished!

All they left behind were huge footprints in the snow!

ANGELS ON ASSIGNMENT

What did angels do between those times of recorded appearances . . . did they rest . . . or what happened to them?

"We are busy all the time scattering God's enemies and putting the pieces of his plan together . . . I commanded a heavenly army with orders from God to push the walls of Jericho into the ground . . . and we did!"

That's what Chrioni, the great warring angel, told me . . . and more!

CHAPTER 13

ANGELS ON ASSIGNMENT

This is a day of renewed spiritual activity! Strange things are happening! People are being awakened! Enemies of Christ are leaving the enemy camp and are moving over to God's side. New voices are being heard proclaiming the Good News. What we are seeing is evidence that an army from heaven is on the move!

I have heard many testimonies of people who were completely away from God; friends have talked to them, members of the family have talked to them, and others have prayed for them, but they stubbornly resisted God. They would appear to be the least likely ones to come to Jesus, but in God's great plan and purpose he sent word through a divine emissary which turned them around. It's happening in the sports world, the business world, the entertainment world, and the political world! People are turning to God and finding him real. The angelic hosts of heaven are on the move!

The whole study of angels is beautiful! The thirteenth chapter of Judges points out an exciting truth about them. "And the children of Israel did evil again in the sight of the Lord; and the Lord delivered them into the hands of the Philistines forty years. And there was a certain man of Zorah, of the family of the Danites, whose name was Manoah; and his wife was barren, and bare not."

In God's plan book, he had destined these forty years, but during this time, he prepared a family through which he could bring deliverance to the people. "And the angel of the Lord appeared unto the woman, and said unto her, Behold now, thou art barren, and bearest not: but thou shalt conceive, and bear a son. Now therefore beware, I pray thee, and drink not wine nor strong drink, and eat not any unclean thing: For, lo, thou shalt conceive, and bear a son; and no razor shall come on his head: for the child shall be a Nazarite unto God from the womb: and he shall begin to deliver Israel out of the hand of the Philistines.

"Then the woman came and told her husband, saying, A man of God came unto me, and his countenance was like the countenance of an angel of God, very terrible: but I asked him not whence he was, neither told he me his name: But he said unto me, Behold, thou shalt conceive, and bear a son; and now drink no wine nor strong drink, neither eat any unclean thing: for the child shall be a Nazarite to God from the womb to the day of his death.

"Then Manoah entreated the Lord, and said, O my Lord, let the man of God which thou didst send come again unto us, and teach us what we shall do unto the child that shall be born. And God hearkened to the voice of Manoah; and the angel of God came again unto the woman as she sat in the field: but Manoah her husband was not with her. And the woman made haste, and ran, and shewed her husband, and said unto him, Behold, the man hath appeared unto me, that came unto me the other day.

"And Manoah arose, and went after his wife, and came to the man, and said unto him, Art thou the man that spakest unto the woman? And he said, I am.

"And Manoah said, Now let thy words come to pass. How shall we order the child, and how shall we do unto him?

"And the angel of the Lord said unto Manoah, Of all that I said unto the woman let her beware. She may not eat of any thing that cometh of the vine, neither let her drink wine or strong drink, nor eat any unclean thing: all that I commanded her let her observe.

"And Manoah said unto the angel of the Lord, I pray thee, let us detain thee, until we shall have made ready a kid for thee.

"And the angel of the Lord said unto Manoah, Though thou detain me, I will not eat of thy bread: and if thou wilt offer a burnt offering, thou must offer it unto the Lord. For Manoah knew not that he was an angel of the Lord.

"And Manoah said unto the angel of the Lord, What is thy name, that when thy sayings come to pass we may do thee honour?

"And the angel of the Lord said unto him, Why askest thou thus after my name, seeing it is secret?

"So Manoah took a kid with a meat offering, and offered it upon a rock unto the Lord: and the angel did wondrously; and Manoah and his wife looked on. For it came to pass, when the flame went up toward heaven from off the altar, that the angel of the Lord ascended in the flame of the altar. And Manoah and his wife looked on it, and fell on their faces to the ground" (Judges 13:1-20).

This is a beautiful story with truths which are up-to-date and pertinent for us today. God saw to it that the message brought by the angel came to pass.

Angels can take on the appearance of a person, but their image is not necessary for their presence to be there. In this story, the angel appeared so that he could be seen with the natural eyes.

The Bible tells us that the angels are God's messengers and they do his bidding. He gives the signals and calls out the orders to them. For this reason, when Manoah prayed, he said, "God, send the angel." This lesson plainly shows that we are not to pray to angels, nor can we command them to do anything! It also shows that the angel stayed quite some time with them and carried on conversation, even teaching them.

Angels are never to be worshipped. They are so ordained and created that there is no place in their entire being for praise or honor. They are called the hosts of the Lord, and their purpose is to serve the eternal God.

There are many beautiful passages throughout the Bible which relate stories of angels. Because Chrioni had been a part of many of these events, he told me some of these stories, and it made them come alive!

In Joshua 5:13,14, the children of Israel had just crossed over the Jordan and were ready to invade the promised land. Joshua went out and saw a man with a sword in his hand and asked him if he was for the Israelites or for their adversaries.

If an angel were to tell believers today what he told Joshua, they would probably be depressed, because this angel said, "Wrong on both counts! I'm not with your enemies, and I'm not part of your army. I'm part of another army, and I have come with orders from God. Standing all around me and behind me in great and mighty columns, are myriads of angels. You can't see them, Joshua, but there is a host of them, and I'm the captain!"

Because someone asked me if this scripture was referring to Jesus as the angel, I asked Chrioni and he said it was not, because he (Chrioni) was there as the captain of the host of the Lord. When Joshua fell on his face to worship, Chrioni told him to take off his shoes; "for the place whereon thou *standest* is holy" (Josh. 5:15). This is the identical thing the angel of the Lord said to Moses from the burning bush! (Ex. 3:4-5).

Chrioni said that God, in his great plan, had it all mapped out. Jericho was the first city they came to, and with a great victory for God here, the other kings and armies would fear the Israelites and know that God was on their side when they saw a great miracle, so God sent Chrioni with a band of angels and with his orders for Jericho. God knew exactly how the city was going to be conquered!

If we could somehow reach back into time and take a look at God's battle plans for this angelic army, they would probably read something like this: "The children of Israel are our allies. They are going to march around those walls seven days, and the last day they will go around seven times. I have already given them their orders, so we are going to have to coordinate those with what we do here. The priests are to blow their trumpets and the people are to shout at a given signal. When you hear their shout, PUSH THE WALLS DOWN!"

Chrioni told me the angels took their positions on top of those walls, waiting for the shout! Israel didn't even know what was going on, but God did, and the angels did! They waited, and when they heard the shout, every angel who was there pushed with all his might and strength, and the great big thick walls went DOWN into the ground! Those walls were thick enough to build a house on, and if they had tipped over, or had been pushed over, they would still have been a wall, because they were about as thick as they were high! God said to the angels, "Push them *down.*" And the Bible tells us that the walls went down "flat" (Josh. 6:20). They didn't even have to pick their way through cracks and rubble because the walls were pushed DOWN into the ground!

This was an act of the angels. I can visualize Chrioni looking at his orders and noticing a special condition God had made for one little part of this wall. When Rahab protected the two spies sent to observe the promised land, God made a promise to her and assured her that he would protect her and her family. I can just see Chrioni ordering some of his angels to go to that part of the wall and hold it up, while the others pushed down on the rest of the wall!

Someone told me recently that the actual excavation shows the walls were pushed down like an elevator shaft. Think of the pressure the angels put on them! I have also been told that in the archaeological findings of the diggings of old Jericho, there is still evidence of the wall where Rahab's house was. Hallelujah!

This really makes the Bible come alive to know that the angels who helped take care of Jericho are still around and are still working with us under the direction of the Holy Spirit.

God has an eternity full of angels. He is not left without resources, and even though he could do everything himself because he is God, he has angels and people working with him all the time.

The angel of the Lord kept Balaam from cursing Israel! Balaam was tempted to curse Israel for some money, but God told the angel not to let him do it. I can imagine Balaam trying to curse Israel, and every time he started, the angel turned his tongue around, and he blessed them instead. He probably said, "What's the matter with me, am I losing my mind?" Then he would again start to curse, and again it would come out a blessing!

He didn't realize there was a big angel standing there who was putting a different "record" in his mouth, and Israel was blessed! This was so much an order from God that he even made a donkey talk! It really frightened Balaam, and he tried to force the donkey to move, but the donkey was stubborn, so instead he turned around and said, "Balaam, haven't I served you well all these years?"

Why would God ever allow such a story to be put in the Bible? Because it happened! That donkey spoke because of the presence of God's angel, even though he didn't know how to speak!

Here are some scriptures to help us not only know and realize the validity of the fact that angels are with us, but that we might be aware of their presence, and know that we can expect God's help through this army from heaven.

An angel came to Zacharias and Elisabeth with the message that John the baptist would be born (Luke 1:11-20).

The angel Gabriel came to Mary and told her that Jesus, the Son of God, was going to be born to her (Luke 1:26-35). That was God's plan unfolding right on time, as he had prepared, planned, and written down before he ever made the earth.

He allowed just exactly the right amount of time, so that on a given day everything would be in readiness. Jesus presented himself as a sacrifice on the exact day that God intended for him to do it. It was definitely not something that God decided on just a few years before it happened!

He let Daniel take a look over his shoulder and said, "Daniel, I'm going to show you some of my plans. Israel is going to go into captivity for seventy years. When the seventy years are up, there is going to be a decree go out by a king to rebuild Jerusalem. If you would like to start counting and count 483 years, you will discover a man who hasn't even been born yet."

He told of the march of Alexander the great, and about the four generals who would be taking over in place of his four sons because God had it planned that way. "But," he said, "At the end of 483 years, Jesus is going to give his life for the world. He is going to die, not for himself, but for the sins of the world!"

Exactly on time, Jesus died for the sins of the world!

In everything God does, he is telling us he loves us, that he cares for us, that he wants us, and that he will help us!

An angel warned Joseph. "After they were gone, an angel of the Lord appeared to Joseph in a dream. 'Get up and flee to Egypt with the baby and his mother,' the angel said, and stay there until I tell you to return, for King Herod is going to try to kill the child' " (Matt. 2:13 TLB).

After Jesus was baptized in the Jordan River, the Word says, "Then Jesus was led out into the wilderness by the Holy Spirit to be tempted there by Satan. For forty days and forty nights he ate nothing and became very hungry. Then Satan tempted him to get food by changing stones into loaves of bread. 'It will prove you are the Son of God,' he said. But Jesus told him, 'No! For the Scriptures tell us that bread won't feed men's souls: obedience to every word of God is what we need.'

"Then Satan took him to Jerusalem to the roof of the Temple. 'Jump off,' he said, 'and prove you are the Son of God; for the Scriptures declare, "God will send his angels to keep you from harm," . . . they will prevent you from smashing on the rocks below.' Jesus retorted, 'It also says not to put the Lord your God to a foolish test!'

"Next Satan took him to the peak of a very high mountain and showed him the nations of the world and all their glory. 'I'll give it all to you,' he said, 'If you will only kneel and worship me.' 'Get out of here, Satan,' Jesus told him. 'The Scriptures say, "Worship only the Lord God. Obey only him.' "

"Then Satan went away, and angels came and cared for Jesus" (Matthew 4:1-11 TLB).

In Luke 22:43 we also read that an angel from heaven came down and strengthened Jesus and ministered to him at the Mount of Olives in his hour of need.

Angels are mentioned throughout the Bible from Genesis to Revelation. In Genesis 24:7, God sent forth an angel to get a bride for Isaac. This was another part of God's plan. In Exodus 23:20 he sent "an Angel before thee, to keep thee in the way, and to bring thee into the place which I have prepared." He sent his angels to clear the way in the going forth out of Egypt.

In Psalm 34:7, the Holy Spirit had David write these words, "The angel of the Lord encampeth round about them that fear him, and delivereth them."

Think of Daniel when he was thrown into the lion's den (Daniel 6:22). The king felt sure that Daniel would be eaten up and there would be nothing but scraps down there in the morning. The king didn't sleep that night, because he was tormented about the thoughts of Daniel being eaten by those vicious lions. He thought about the horrible thing he had done by throwing Daniel into the lion's den, so the first thing in the morning, he ran and looked in and cried out, "Oh, Daniel, servant of the Living God, was your God, whom you worship continually, able to deliver you from the lions?" "Did he do it?" He really didn't expect an answer back, but he thought he would try anyway. "My God has sent his angel," he said, "to shut the lions' mouths so that they can't touch me" (Dan. 6:20,22 TLB).

The angels of God are mighty! Since they are performing the work of God, they are unlimited in power. If one single angel could do so much, think of what the hosts of heaven that are marching today can do! Think of what they can accomplish. In every case, as the plan of God was unfolding and another chapter was being opened, the angels of God became visible and brought messages, and in our day, people all over the world have had visits from visible angels.

This ought to tell us something. God isn't letting this world run down without His notice and His attention. Another chapter is unfolding! Jesus is about ready to come! Hallelujah! The greatest rescue mission ever accomplished in all of the universe is about ready to take place. He has His angels out working now. They haven't just appeared in rare instances, but reports are being received all over the country that angelic beings are being seen!

I was thrilled when a Christian brother, John Weaver, told me about how he was visited twice by an angel.

"As I was fixing my car alongside the road, I saw a car coming right across the plowed field about a quarter of a mile from me. It was a brand new car and the dirt and dust were flying behind it as it came right across a plowed field at me. He drove me into town so I could secure help and then instantly disappeared. I learned later that it was an angel coming to my rescue."

"God visited me in a very special way again in 1971 and spoke to me about the work I was to do for Him. At this point in time in my ministry and my spiritual development, God in His grace saw fit to send the same angel to speak to me once again who had helped me approximately twenty years earlier.

"It was wintertime in Montana and some friends and I went hunting for elk...I was two-thirds of the way to the top of the ridge where I was headed when I saw a man coming out of the trees on the next ridge near the timberline. He did not have on Hunter orange and was walking right down to me without carrying a gun. He seemed to be walking at the same pace a normal man would walk, but he covered the ground between us so quickly...in a matter of seconds! I noticed that as he walked, HE LEFT NO FOOTPRINTS IN THE SNOW!

"The man walked up to me and shook my hand. He said 'John, do you know who I am?' I responded, speaking out of my spirit, 'Yes, you are a servant of the Lord.' He said, 'Yes, that is right. The Lord has sent me here today to talk with you.' We sat down on two big rocks facing each other. It was not until later that I realized I was talking with the same angel who had helped me when my car broke down twenty years earlier!

"We talked about how God was pleased that I had moved my prayer life from a selfish prayer to one of compassion for those around me, and among other things, about needing a house for my family...at that point the angel stopped me! This was the first time he had said anything since I had begun sharing with him. He said, 'How much money do you need?' I said, 'Maybe $20,000.'

"The angel said, 'You know that I could give you that $20,000 in hundred dollar bills right now, don't you?' Somehow I knew he could do it, so I replied, 'Yes.' He said, 'We don't do things that way, though. The Lord puts it upon the hearts of His people. That money will be taken care of and you don't have to tell anyone. It will just come in.' He talked with me twenty or thirty minutes more, telling me some beautiful truths and some exciting things about how it would be in eternity in heaven. What a thrill!

"I was amazed at what the angel had said, but I became more amazed as he began to share some principles that were to change my life. The angel said, 'John, you have a ministry that is eternal. It is not just earthly, it is eternal! The little things that you are doing now, your ministry and your faithfulness now, are going to determine your destiny of tomorrow, your ministry of tomorrow. To the degree that you will humble yourself and minister under His direction, you will be just what God wants you to be.'

"Another thing he said was, 'God has given you alternatives and allowed you to make choices. You can choose to be close to Him and be used by Him or you can go your own way, do your own thing and live a selfish life. What you do here and the choices you make here will all be reflected in your relationship with God when you get to heaven. You will realize that there are not just crowns put on your head, but there will be rewards of relationship and ministry being given to you also. If you will be faithful here, God will give you an increased ministry there.

"Two weeks later, I was driving back from a meeting, worshipping the Lord in the car and thinking about the $20,000 the angel had mentioned. Suddenly, I felt the Lord's presence in the car right beside me. Whether it was the angel again speaking for the Lord, or the Lord speaking directly I do not know. He spoke to me about the $20,000, reminding me that I had never asked for it. When I replied by asking, He said, 'Starting tomorrow morning, that money is going to come in.' And just like that, it was as though he slipped out of the moving car and was gone!'"

The Bible tells us that God hasn't changed. The Word says that people have entertained strangers and were not aware that they were angels. You don't always know them when you see them, unless you happen to see them step into a fire and go up in a flame, jump out of a car when it's moving and not hit the ground, or wake you in the middle of the night, but they are around.

Not one of the angels have ever died. They have not decreased in strength, they are still mighty! They have been sent forth to help us, to provide and care for us, and to camp around us. Psalm 91:11 says He has given them charge over us. They come as fast as the command of God or the thought of God. They may appear as an ordinary man of the street, they may appear as a dim, almost invisible figure, or they may appear as distinct a person as you or I. But one thing you can be sure of, you can clearly distinguish the difference between the real angels and your imagination. You don't have to struggle to see them to know they are there. They will make it plain that they are real angels, if that is their mission.

The angels prepare the way for us just as they prepared the way for people in the Bible. God wants us to be aware of the fact that He is not helpless in a corner somewhere, but His angels have been sent forth with the assignment to take care of His people.

"After testifying and preaching in Samaria, Peter and John returned to Jerusalem...But as for Philip, an angel of the Lord said to him, 'Go over to the road that runs from Jerusalem through the Gaza Desert, arriving around noon.'" (Acts 8:25-27 TLB). What was the purpose of the angel telling him to go over there? So he could meet the Ethiopian eunuch and introduce him to Jesus! God is doing the same thing today!

It would be exciting to see what the angels are doing right now in relation to your unsaved loved ones. You might think that nothing in heaven or earth could move them and turn them toward God, but there are angels out there tugging at them and following them along, because God wants them to be His. Angels are on special assignment from God to help you and your friends and relatives find Him!

God loves us enough that He has prepared everything that we need for our deliverance and our help. He has sent His Holy Spirit to be with us, to teach us, and watch over us. The angels encamp around us! How can we lose?

Angels are on assignment today! Hallelujah!

HE IS COMING AGAIN!

. . . As I think of the return of Jesus, I remember what Gabriel said, "There has never been such excitement and activity in the courts of heaven since Jesus came the first time, as there is right now!"

CHAPTER 14

HE IS COMING AGAIN!

Where are we on God's calendar?

If man's stay on earth from the time of Adam and Eve could be placed into a clock with twelve hours, I believe we would be right at the end of the eleventh hour, ready for the clock to strike twelve! There are many indications that we are rapidly moving close to the end of time as we know it!

Jesus is coming! He didn't say when, but he did tell us we can know the times and the seasons. We can know the seasons because each one has individual indications of when it is coming. When spring comes, the grass starts turning green and the little roots start putting out their shoots. When summer comes, the flowers bloom. When fall arrives, everything turns orange and brown. Winter brings the cold and snow. You can see the evidence and know what season it is.

How much time is left, we don't know, but we do know this, that God has permitted each of us to live in the greatest and most exciting days of all history . . . days when people around the world are responding to God and to what he is doing. People from all faiths, from all walks of life and from all nationalities are hearing the call and they are waking up!

People are discovering that the most important thing we can stand on is the eternal, everlasting Word of God! A growing hunger is being created in hearts all over the world for a greater understanding of God's promises. People are learning that God will never violate his character and he will never violate his Word!

"I go to prepare a place for you. And if I go and prepare a place for you, I will come again, and receive you unto myself; that where I am, there ye may be also" (John 14:2,3). JESUS SAID HE WAS COMING AGAIN!

"And there shall be signs in the sun, and in the moon, and in the stars; and upon the earth distress of nations, with perplexity; the sea and the waves roaring; Men's hearts failing them for fear, and for looking after those things which are coming on the earth: for the powers of heaven shall be shaken. And then shall they see the Son of man coming in a cloud with power and great glory. And when these things begin to come to pass, then look up, and lift up your heads; for your redemption draweth nigh" (Luke 21:25-28).

"And while they looked stedfastly toward heaven as he went up, behold, two men stood by them in white apparel; Which also said, Ye men of Galilee, why stand ye gazing up into heaven? this same Jesus, which is taken up from you into heaven, shall so come in like manner as ye have seen him go into heaven" (Acts 1:10,11).

Angelic beings visited the earth when Jesus was here. They are visiting the earth today!

Did you notice that the angels said, "This same Jesus?" Angels are talking today, just as they did then, and are bringing the good news that he is coming! This same Jesus is coming back to earth! I certainly don't know how or when, but I definitely know that he IS! God has an eternity full of secrets he hasn't told us anything about, but one thing he has made clear is that Jesus is coming!

The disciples felt a genuine urgency about preparing for the second coming of the Lord. They looked forward to the time when ". . . the Lord himself will come down from heaven with a mighty shout and with the soul-stirring cry of the archangel and the great trumpet-call of God" (I Thes. 4:16 TLB).

Paul told us that if you believe Jesus died, and arose from the dead, you also have to believe that he is coming again! He encouraged us to "comfort one another with these words" (I Thes. 4:18). We have something exciting to talk about to other people! When you see them looking down, say, "Cheer up, Jesus is coming!"

We find this positive belief many places in Paul's writings. He said part of the Good News is that God is taking care of things so you won't have to worry and be in a constant frenzy, wondering whether or not you are going to be ready when Jesus comes. There may be a lot of ups and downs on the path, but if you have linked arms with Jesus and are serving him, you are in God's family, and he will keep "your spirit and soul and body strong and blameless until that day when our Lord Jesus Christ comes back again. God, who called you to become his child, will do all this for you, just as he promised" (I Thes. 5:23,24 TLB).

One of the most beautiful things about these messages the angels are bringing from God's heart is that they are making it possible for people to find new victories. They can relax, stop struggling and let his life flow through them. That flow-through of his life will take care of all the problems and situations that are troubling you. When we keep our eyes on the answer, which is Jesus, instead of the problem, we will find it easy to let his life flow through us.

James talked about it in the fifth chapter, verses seven and eight, "Be patient therefore, brethren, unto the coming of the Lord. Behold, the husbandman waiteth for the precious fruit of the earth, and hath long patience for it, until he receive the early and latter rain. Be ye also patient; stablish your hearts: for the coming of the Lord draweth nigh." He may not come when you think he is going to, because there are some things he must still accomplish, but be patient, HE IS COMING!

Peter talked about it and spoke of the time when Jesus would be revealed from heaven. In I Peter 1:13 he says that you can stop worrying now and rest secure in the knowledge that Jesus is bringing with him a special load of grace when he comes. We don't need to look at the weaknesses, the hurts and the hard times around, we need to start looking for that special grace which is going to be brought to us at the appearing of Jesus Christ when he is revealed from heaven. "And this is the secret: that Christ in your hearts is your only hope of glory" (Col. 1:27 TLB).

John spoke of the return of Jesus in I John 3:2, where he said it doesn't yet appear what we shall be, but we know that when he appears, something is going to happen! "...We shall be like him; for we shall see him as he is!"

Jude spoke of his coming back to earth in the 24th verse where he said, "Now unto him that is able to keep you from falling, and to present you faultless before the presence of his glory with exceeding joy." Jude believed it, and he was encouraging people to quit worrying about falling. God is big enough to call you, to help you, and to deliver you of your sins.

All the markers of history tell us that he is coming! Social standards, indicating the increased activity of Satan, the physical signs upon this earth, and the great spiritual moves that we are seeing, all point to the return of Jesus! There is no question about it. Something is happening today in the spiritual realm of the world, and we are a living part of it!

As I think of the return of Jesus, I vividly remember those soul-stirring words that Gabriel said, "There has never been such excitement and activity in the courts of heaven since Jesus came the first time, as there is right now!"

MARANATHA, COME LORD JESUS SOON!

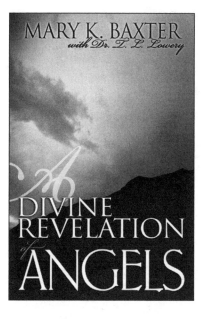

A Divine Revelation of Angels

Mary K. Baxter
with Dr. T. L. Lowery

Best-selling author Mary Baxter describes dreams, visions, and revelations of angels that God has given her. Explore the fascinating dynamics of angelic beings—their appearance, their assigned functions and roles, and how they operate, not only in the heavenly realms, but also in our lives here on earth. God's holy angels are magnificent beings who are His messengers and warriors sent to assist, protect, and deliver us through the power of Christ.

ISBN: 978-0-88368-866-3 • Trade • 288 pages

www.whitakerhouse.com

The Power of Faith
Smith Wigglesworth

Need a miracle? God has one for you.
Trapped in poverty? Access God's unlimited resources.
Lack vision and purpose? Discover your God-given destiny.
Feel powerless? God wants to use you in amazing ways.

Laughing at the impossible was a way of life for Smith Wigglesworth.
He trusted wholeheartedly in the words of Jesus, "Only believe."
God used a simple faith to restore sight to the blind, health to the
sick, even life to the dead. This same kind of miracle-working faith
can be yours. As you believe God, your faith will explode.
Your miracle is waiting for you—dare to believe.

ISBN: 978-0-88368-608-9 • Trade • 544 pages

WHITAKER
HOUSE
www.whitakerhouse.com